MY SOUL

PRAISE FOR WATER MY SOUL

"Water My Soul *is a lovely collection of real events that whisk the mind to a beautiful way of life, while the insights resonate with the longings from the deepest part of our hearts.*"
—CINDY WOODSMALL, *NEW YORK TIMES* BESTSELLING AUTHOR OF AMISH FICTION

"*I felt as though I were taking a walk with a wise fellow mother through her well-kept garden. I enjoyed the way Darla lifts actual stories from her family life and gardening experiences to guide my thoughts toward devotion to the One who can truly water the soul. With down-to-earth illustrations and pertinent questions, Darla invited me to worship the Master Gardener with her.*"
—SHEILA PETRE, AUTHOR OF *FROM JOY TO JOY* AND *THIRTY LITTLE FINGERS* AND EDITOR OF *THE KING'S DAUGHTER*

"*Darla Weaver has created a candid collection of simple devotions, many of them centered on anecdotes gleaned from gardening and family life. Each story is beautifully connected to biblical truths, a prayer, and a reflective question.*"
—LINDA MAENDEL, AUTHOR OF *HUTTERITE DIARIES: WISDOM FROM MY PRAIRIE COMMUNITY*

"*What a great book of inspiration! Reading a chapter or two of this book each morning starts my day out on the right path. It will give many busy mothers encouragement for the day.*"
—LOVINA EICHER, AUTHOR OF *THE ESSENTIAL AMISH COOKBOOK* AND THE SYNDICATED NEWSPAPER COLUMN, LOVINA'S AMISH KITCHEN

"*These devotional readings provide glimpses of the presence of God that is all around us if we only open our eyes and see.*"
—MARY ANN KINSINGER, *A JOYFUL CHAOS* BLOGGER, AND CO-AUTHOR OF THE ADVENTURES OF LILY LAPP SERIES

water MY SOUL

90 Meditations from an
Old Order Mennonite

DARLA WEAVER

Herald Press
Harrisonburg, Virginia

Library of Congress Cataloging-in-Publication Data

Names: Weaver, Darla, author.
Title: Water my soul : ninety meditations from an old order Mennonite / Darla
  Weaver.
Description: Harrisonburg : Herald Press, 2017. I Series: Plainspoken
  devotional I Includes bibliographical references.
Identifiers: LCCN 2017003435I ISBN 9781513802411 (pbk. : alk. paper) I ISBN
  9781513802428 (hardcover : alk. paper)
Subjects: LCSH: Christian life--Old Order Mennonite authors--Meditations. I
  Christian women--Religious life--Meditations.
Classification: LCC BV4501.3 .W387 2017 I DDC 242--dc23 LC record available at
  https://lccn.loc.gov/2017003435

WATER MY SOUL
© 2017 by Herald Press, Harrisonburg, Virginia 22802. 800-245-7894.
All rights reserved.
Library of Congress Control Number: 2017003435
International Standard Book Number: 978-1-5138-0241-1 (paperback);
  978-1-5138-0242-8 (hardcover); 978-1-5138-0243-5 (ebook)
Printed in United States of America
Cover and interior design by Reuben Graham

Unless otherwise noted, Scripture text is quoted with permission from the *King
James Version*.

21 20 19 18 17   10 9 8 7 6 5 4 3 2 1

TO LAVERNE: Thank you for seventeen happy years.

CONTENTS

Acknowledgments **9**
A Day in the Life of the Author **10**

WEEK 1: LESSONS FROM NATURE

1. Barren Soil **14** | 2. Preparing Soil **16**
3. Sending Down Roots **18** | 4. Winter Hope **20**
5. Children and Gardens **22** | 6. Even Earthworms **24**
7. Winter Storm **26**

WEEK 2: WHERE FERNS GROW NOW

1. From Scars to Ferns **28** | 2. Cody's Flower **30**
3. Procrastination **32** | 4. Children and Doctors **34**
5. Your Speech Betrays You **36** | 6. Sticking Out **38**
7. Small Beginnings **40**

WEEK 3: CHOCOLATE-COVERED STORIES AND BASEBALL BATS

1. Chocolate and Stories **42** | 2. Differences **44**
3. Contentment and Baseball Bats **46** | 4. Winter Homecoming **48**
5. What Time I Am Afraid **50** | 6. The Results of Pain **52**
7. Corinthians Today **54**

WEEK 4: THE FALLS OF LIFE

1. This Is Faith 56 | 2. Decisions 58
3. Falls of Life 60 | 4. Jumping Ship 62
5. Dangerous Powers 64 | 6. A New Jerusalem 66
7. "I'm Better'n You!" 68

WEEK 5: POWERFUL PRUNING

1. Blueberry the Cat 70 | 2. Sowing Ferns, Reaping Wisteria 72
3. The Dash Between 74 | 4. Obedience 76
5. Happiness Is 78 | 6. Soul Gardening 80
7. More Pruning 82

WEEK 6: JOY REQUIRES TENDING

1. Pruning Hearts 84 | 2. Service 86
3. Improvements 88 | 4. Gratitude and Beetles 90
5. Old Faithfuls 92 | 6. Lettuce or Roses or Weeds 94
7. Hydrangea Flowers 96

WEEK 7: STILL MY RESTLESS LONGING

1. Matthan's Water 98 | 2. Houses That Last 100
3. Doing God's Will 102 | 4. Working for the Lord 104
5. Faith through the Fiery Furnace 106 | 6. The Faith Chapter 108
7. Job's Faith 110

WEEK 8: THE MUNDANE AND THE MOMENTOUS

1. Job's Hope 112 | 2. Broken Hearts, Part 1 114
3. Broken Hearts, Part 2 116 | 4. Waiting 118
5. The Folded Napkin 120 | 6. For One Single Day 122
7. A Daylily in November 124

WEEK 9: HEARING GOD

1. Forgiveness of Flowers 126 | 2. Bearing Fruit 128
3. Pressing On 130 | 4. Our Thoughts 132
5. Plugged Ears 134 | 6. Unplugging My Ears to Hear God 136
7. Who Are the Saints? 138

WEEK 10: WHEN WE FAIL

1. A Heavenly Parent 140 | 2. Peter's Mistakes 142
3. Peter's Question 144 | 4. When Peter Was Sleeping 146
5. Courage 148 | 6. Small Things 150
7. Failure and Success 152

WEEK 11: LIVING FOR CHRIST

1. Submission 154 | 2. Peacemakers 156
3. Birth and Growth 158 | 4. Rocks and Clay and Briars 160
5. Fading Flowers 162 | 6. Going Out Blooming 164
7. Rest 166

WEEK 12: THE PATH OF PAIN

1. Tails in the Toilet 168 | 2. Treasures 170
3. The Path of Pain 172 | 4. Counterfeits 174
5. Master and King 176 | 6. Winding Lane 178
7. A Servant's Heart 180

WEEK 13: HEADING HOME

1. Such as We Judge 182 | 2. Children and God's Children 184
3. Where Safety Is 186 | 4. Harvest 188
5. The Story of Two Apple Trees 190 | 6. Pruning Back the Forest 192
7. Life's Crossroads 194

FAQs about Old Order Mennonites: The Author Answers 196
Notes 198
About the Author 200

ACKNOWLEDGMENTS

I love God, my family, and our way of living our faith as part of an Old Order Mennonite community in southern Ohio. I also like working with plants and words, and writing this book has been a unique way of combining everything I love.

Several people have helped me a great deal in all the steps necessary to take this book from its beginning to its conclusion, and it seems only fair to acknowledge that assistance with a grateful thank you.

The editors at Herald Press—Valerie Weaver-Zercher, who suggested this project and got it started, and Melodie Davis, who saw it through to the end. Melodie, you were always there to answer my questions and help me along, and your editing expertise polished my words.

My friends Glen and Ida Rose Martin, who kindly read the entire first draft of this manuscript and shared their thoughts and encouragement.

My friend Faith Sommers, whose prayers and encouragement were a bright spot in the early days as I struggled to get this manuscript up and running.

And always, always, a special thank you to Laverne, who not only supports my writing but encourages it, and to our children, Cody, Alisha, Matthan. You are familiar with all the hazards that go with having a wife and mother who writes—yet you continue to love me anyway.

A DAY IN THE LIFE OF THE AUTHOR

Monday, November 7, 2016

6:00 A.M.
The alarm is supposed to wake us at six. This morning it doesn't. When we tried to get it to acknowledge the end of daylight saving time yesterday, it refused. Either it has acquired a mind of its own or it's worn out. But we're awake when it's time to get up anyhow.

When I go upstairs to call Cody, his bed is empty. I find him sleeping outside on the balcony, where he has moved an extra mattress, some blankets, and sleeping bags. Although our nights have been fairly mild so far, I guess there's a certain novelty in sleeping outside in November.

"This is the 'Day in the life of the author,'" I tell my family while they eat breakfast. "I'll be writing about you today."

No one comments.

"I guess we're used to it," Laverne says after a while.

7:45 A.M.
Morning work and breakfast are over, except for Matthan, who is five and is eating a bowlful of wheat puffs and pretending to share every other spoonful with a toy duck. Laverne is at the woodworking shop at his dad's place a short distance down the lane. Cody, who is fourteen and graduated from school this spring, is helping at the finishing shop at our place today. He and one of the employees are staining an order of trim and doors.

And Alisha is off to school. She packed her lunch and fed her fat and spoiled quartet of cats, and I combed and braided her hair before she left. She is twelve and in seventh grade at Fairview School two and a half miles away. Our church community has five schools, each with two rooms and two teachers. One also has a small special education classroom.

10:00 A.M.

It's a beautifully mild morning, and Monday's many loads of laundry have filled the lines. Now I have time for a brief coffee break, and Matthan joins me for a small snack. Then I will cook a kettleful of sweet potatoes and work at deep-cleaning Alisha's bedroom until it's time to prepare our lunch.

11:30 A.M.

Lunchtime. Matthan sets the table and Laverne and Cody come in from the shop. By twelve thirty our meal is over, the dishes are washed, and the men have gone back to work. Today Matthan runs along to the shop to play.

The next hours are some of my favorite of the day—I spend them at my desk. Today I don't have to wonder what to write, but rather which manuscript to work on. Besides this one, I'm also working on the first draft of book 3 in a series, and my brother has given me the first five chapters of a book he is writing about his experiences thru-hiking the Appalachian Trail that he wants me to edit. So I can't wash the dishes fast enough to get to the sunny little room off the kitchen where I have my desk and scores of Matthan's toys. When it's cold outside he surrounds my desk with toy farms and animals, trucks, blocks, trike, bike, and scooter.

3:15 P.M.

Before I know what has happened, it's after three o'clock. Alisha is home from school, and it's time to have a snack and look at the mail before we start our afternoon's work. Together we put away the laundry, and I make a casserole for tomorrow. My four sisters and I spend almost every Tuesday with Mom, and we bring part of the noon meal. Alisha gathers supplies for a Christmas card–making period they'll have at school tomorrow. That is something they do each year, and the cards are mailed to jails and distributed among the prisoners.

6:00 P.M.

Suppertime. For us it works best to have our devotions in the evening, and we are ready to begin reading the Gospel according to John, chapter 1. This is perhaps the best time of the day, when everyone is home again and evening begins. In the winter, our evenings are spent reading, writing, talking, and playing various games. Laverne usually puts in several hours doing shop work after the four horses, one cow, and flocks of hens are fed.

8:30 P.M.

I help Matthan get ready for bed. The older children go down at nine. Then I can settle in the recliner and read for another hour until our bedtime.

But often I fall asleep instead!

Good night.

1

BARREN SOIL

Mark 4:1-20

*W*hen we, as newlyweds, first came to our home at Mountain Lane Acres, it was just that: bare acres of land on top of a mountain accessed by a long lane. That lane wound a rambling, almost mile-long journey along the side of the mountain. The hillside that sloped down over the mountain was strewn with rocks of all sizes, from pebbles to boulders, and no soil was visible. It was all covered by woodland plants and fallen leaves. And rocks.

Being optimistic, my husband and I plowed up a small square of hilltop land that first spring and planted a garden. Here, at least, there were no rocks. A thin layer resembling topsoil was upended, but most of the overturned sod had an odd orange hue. It was, we were to learn that summer, about 96 percent clay. The remaining 4 percent wasn't all that great either.

As I said, we were optimistic—and blissfully naive. We chopped up great clods of rust-colored soil and made rows down the length of the garden. We bought seeds and planted them, covering each one with more of the small hard lumps that were "soil." Then we hung up the hoe and sat back to watch our garden grow.

We learned a few things about clay that year. One was to recognize its unyielding, brick-like substance when it was dry. And also it refused to drain. When it rained, water collected in the flat areas on top of our hill and pooled there for days. Clay, we learned, was rock-hard and full of clods only half the time. For the other, it became waterlogged and reverted to a smeary mud that stuck to everything.

The plants that tried to grow never did get very far that first summer. Some drowned where puddles collected, others turned yellow and took on a sickly appearance. The few that managed to survive were too stressed to yield much in the way of vegetables.

When I planted my first garden, I had no way of knowing how much I still needed to learn. I never guessed how much hard work was still ahead of me.

And when I first decided to accept Jesus as my Savior and as the Lord and Master of my life, to become a baptized disciple of Christ and a member of a Bible-believing church, I had no way of knowing how much I had yet to learn. In many ways, my heart still resembled that clay soil. Hard, barren, and unyielding. There were some pretty big clods in my heart garden that would have to be broken up before I could begin to bring forth much fruit.

Gardening became a journey of learning. Sure, I had grown up on a farm. But I never gave the soil a second glance nor realized that healthy dirt is the lifeblood of a thriving farm. I set out to learn all the ways I could improve the soil in my garden.

Patterning one's life after the life of Jesus is also an ongoing journey of discovery. As I worked in my ever-expanding gardens, I was amazed how often God used the natural world to open my eyes to new spiritual truths. Looking back now—fifteen years later—I can see that I have learned much. But I can see even more clearly how much I still have to learn.

Some days I find it exciting. There's an element of surprise and discovery in wondering what new things I will unearth in my gardens. What new things will God teach in the details of life?

Other days, it looks like too much work and a lot of digging in the dirt. The effort required for beautiful gardens—earth gardens or heart gardens—is too much.

But even when I would give up, God does not. And always, always, the results are worth the toil.

Prayer

Please continue to work in the barren places of my heart, Lord. Even the hard, stony places are full of potential when surrendered to you.

Reflection

How could I use today to grow closer to the One who wants to make my heart a beautiful garden?

2

PREPARING SOIL

Mark 4:21-34

*W*hen a second growing season arrived at our hilltop home, I knew two things. First, I wanted a vegetable garden and more flowers. Second, the soil needed amendments. If I wanted rich, black garden dirt, I'd have to make some. It obviously wasn't going to appear on its own.

I wasn't even smart enough in those days to know about all the bagged and packaged soil improvements available at garden centers that would increase the health of my soil. But we had one thing available, and we used it a lot: horse manure. We cleaned out the barn and worked loads of it into the square of sod that was the vegetable garden. It was smelly sometimes, and dirty always, but it was necessary.

It all helped, but it took a few more seasons and a lot more work until the garden began to improve. Gradually, I started to understand that the key to beautiful plants was beautiful soil, and I didn't have any of my own worth speaking of. All of it had to be made, and it was going to take a long time. This was a lifelong journey, and one that would demand much of me.

But I did notice that the soil was changing. The orange tint was replaced by dark brown and black, and there were no hard clods. Each season the earth was softer and blacker, more moist and deep, and there were more earthworms. It was slowly becoming rich and tillable. I could now plant a seed and expect it to grow and yield good fruit.

I had added manure and mulch and shredded leaves to the gardens. Plus straw and grass clippings, compost and more mulch.

Months and then years had come and gone, and as they slipped away they left a gardener's dream soil in place of that ugly clay. I'd done my part; the years had done theirs. Together we'd crafted a soil where plants could flourish.

I didn't realize it initially, but as I worked in the gardens I was designing, God was working in my heart. It came gradually, so slowly that at first I wasn't quite aware of it. He was designing a garden too, a heart garden to bring him delight in the same way my gardens delighted me.

He was using the details of my life to craft this garden, and the disappointments fit into his plan, as well as the happy occurrences.

It took divine wisdom and patience to use the ugly parts of my life as well as the good: the things that turned out wrong—the heart-aches and discouragements—as part of the design for improvement. But it was all necessary. By using both the light and the dark, the sorrow and the joy, he was creating a kind of soil in my heart that was becoming softer and more pliable and ready to be planted with more of his seeds of faith.

Obviously, a heart to bring glory to its Creator wasn't going to happen on its own, and it wasn't going to happen in a single season. But the more I learned about God and the way he was working in my life, the more I was able to love and honor him. Even the murky, hard places, the trials that were so difficult at the time, served a purpose in his plans for my life.

Prayer

Lord, I understand that I must prepare the soil in my gardens if I want my plants to grow well. And I realize that my heart must be prepared too, so your Word can flourish there.

Reflection

What was one disappointment in my life that now, looking back, I can see that God turned into something good?

3

SENDING DOWN ROOTS

Mark 4:35-41

Late winter, just before the warming earth starts coaxing new growth to begin, is prime time to transplant shrubs and perennials. Some have outgrown their old space, some aren't thriving where I'd planted them, and some I just want to grow elsewhere. I do a lot of rearranging in the flower gardens.

The plants I'm digging up might be tall or squat, prickly or soft, miniature or enormous. But they all have one thing in common. Roots, of vast or hairlike proportions, burrow deep into the black depths of the earth.

They have another thing in common too. They protest mightily about being torn from their cozy nest in the shelter of the soil. The deeper they grow, the harder I have to work. I use a shovel and force the pile of knotted roots upward out of the ground.

And there, exposed, is the network that anchors the stalk into the earth. The most vital part of any plant. Hidden in the depths of the soil, these roots absorb nutrients and moisture. They are the source of life. Healthy roots will grow healthy leaves and flowers and food. Roots that are shallow and sick will produce growth that looks sick. There's really no way for sick roots to grow healthy plants.

When I improved the health of my soil, the roots automatically became larger and healthier. Not only was the part above ground flourishing, but so also was the part beneath the surface. And the unseen part was where the source of life was located.

I knew that, deep within my heart, God had carefully prepared the soil for his garden, and then he had sown his seeds. He had done his part. Now it was up to me. I had to make room in my life for his Word, to make time to read, hear, and think about it.

Those roots in my life must go deep too, down to where no one but God can see. He uses his inspired word in the Bible; he uses the tempests and trials around me, the droughts and floods and frosts, to teach me how to grow. Roots anchored deep in the Word of God, a heart anchored to faith and trust, will help me to stand strong when storms come. They are the most vital part of a Christian's life: that network of faith and prayer, trust and discipleship. We must have roots that anchor our lives to God's love and his plan.

Yet if I allowed weeds to choke out my plants, it wouldn't matter how good the soil was; any crops I hoped to harvest would be ruined. If I allowed all the duties and demands of daily life to smother the seeds God planted, the garden he desired in my life would die too.

Healthy roots allow me to absorb the source of life that God provides. The more I read about God and that divine love for all, the more I marvel about the beautiful world he has created for us, and the more the roots in my heart grow deeper and stronger.

Prayer

I'm still learning about you, God, and the more I learn, the more I marvel. Continue to open my eyes, and teach me more of what you have planned for me.

Reflection

How much time have I planned to spend with God today?

4

WINTER HOPE

1 Corinthians 9:10; Psalm 33:22

One midwinter day that was pleasantly mild, I headed outdoors with my pruning shears. It was exactly the kind of day I
needed to begin tidying the flower gardens for spring.

Long, undulating lines of brown stalks rose from the frozen earth
of the garden near the woods, and they all fell as I chopped. With-
ered canes of last year's coneflowers, daisies, goosenecks, liatris,
lilies, old-fashioned hydrangeas, and lamb's ears all tumbled to the
ground. I gathered great piles of dead foliage and hauled it away. It
was such a satisfying feeling to watch the backbone of the garden
emerge and to see neat lines where there had been dead and unkempt
confusion just moments before.

Yet as I worked, I became aware that the gardens were not as
dead and frozen as I had thought. Just above the roots of the plants
was the hope of spring in the form of young growth. Taking away
the tall stalks of dead sedums, I uncovered tiny green leaves about
the size of my little fingernail. At the base of the masses of lavender,
obedient plants were a few slim green leaves waiting to become this
spring's new growth. Here was the hope of spring and of new life.

The gardens were still frozen with winter, and they certainly
looked dead, but it was only for a short time. Below the surface,
underneath the frost line, and deep in the soil, was abundant life. It
was just waiting until the time was right to bloom.

Sometimes our hearts experience winter too, and everything
seems to be frozen and dead. But often that which appears to be an
end is simply a new beginning.

Deep in the frozen soil of our hearts lies latent life, waiting for sunshine to thaw it and for the right moment to unfurl new growth. Winter is the time God has designed for plants to rest before a season of profusion and abundance. The growth is hidden now, but it is there all the same, and it goes deep.

Winter in our hearts can be the same—a season of regrouping, of learning to burrow deeper into the soil, of being still and waiting for God's plan to unfold in our lives. Amid bleakness, pain, sorrow, surrender, and distress, God can teach us most about life and himself. It is in times of regrouping that we reach out to him most often.

The frozen bleakness of winter in the garden always ends at last in spring. And a heart that was frozen by winter's sorrow will move on too. Hope flourishes even in the dark seasons, and it blooms once more when the sun shines again.

Prayer

Some sorrows are so all-consuming that it seems they will never end. But you have promised, Lord, that it passes and does not stay, and I look with hope toward a brighter day.

Reflection

What is one situation in my life in which I should wait to see what God is doing before I move on?

5

CHILDREN AND GARDENS

Mark 10:13-16; 3 John 4

*W*hen the children arrived to call us Daddy and Mom, they added a new dimension not only to our lives but also to my gardens. Mostly to the garden God was developing within my heart, but later also to the gardens outside the four walls of our home.

Cody arrived first, a dark-eyed, dark-haired little charmer. Laverne liked to hold him and quote lines from Longfellow's poem "Hiawatha's Childhood": "Who is this, that lights the wigwam? / With his great eyes lights the wigwam? / Ewa-yea! my little owlet!"

Two years later, Alisha arrived. She was as blond of hair and blue of eyes as Cody was dark, and we were delighted to have a daughter. She was a genuinely happy little girl.

For seven years, they were the two who grew up alongside the flowers. They were the two who taught me more about God's love for me than any other single thing ever did. They taught me more about trust too. It takes a lot of faith to believe God will take care of our most precious possessions and to know that he loves them even more than we do.

Seven years and two months later, Matthan arrived. His name is of Hebrew origin and means "gift of God." He has been exactly that, this surprise package God knew we needed. He is a pleasant little fellow who is the delight of our lives.

So here were more gardens, of a different sort, given into my care. Children's hearts resemble gardens to me, places where the things I plant, the good and the bad alike, grow.

The children didn't have to grow much before I could see myself in them. What's more, I could also hear myself. Oh, I heard myself all right, over and over. One can seldom find better mimics or copycats than children. Their young minds soak up almost everything. Every seed I planted took root and began to grow. The soil in their little hearts wasn't clay. It was deep and fertile and ready to be filled with seeds that would grow. I was only discovering that what I planted there would also reflect who I was, and to a great degree.

It was a daunting task. How could God expect me, who was neither very wise nor very old, to be capable of this great responsibility of motherhood?

But God's plan is full of wisdom and as old as time, and it is a good plan. He knew I couldn't be a mother without his help, and he taught me hour by hour as I taught my children. With his help, I learned to be a mother. It was harder to learn to be a mother than a gardener, and yet both jobs were strikingly similar. I was nurturing living things, caring for them by providing healthy food, a pleasant and safe and secure environment, the right kind of assistance and support, and a loving vigil at all times.

Without a doubt, being a gardener was the easier of the two tasks. Also without a doubt, being a mother, while greatly challenging, was the one I loved the best.

Prayer

Lord Jesus, my children are the only things I have that are possible to take along to heaven, and you are the only one who can bridge the gulf and take them there. I place them in your care again today and for the rest of their lives.

Reflection

How can I be a blessing to one other woman today, whether my mother, daughter, sister, or friend?

6

EVEN EARTHWORMS

Isaiah 55

These days, I have two sons and a daughter to help me garden, but Matthan, the youngest at four years, is most eager to do so. Because he doesn't yet consider it work, he likes it all. Even the earthworms.

I didn't yet know it, that first spring when I planted a garden, but the lack of earthworms in that brick-like clay was a sign of a serious deficiency. Earthworms tunnel through soil beneath the mulch, chewing up all sorts of debris. They leave behind worm castings as fertilizer, and make the ground soft and friable. They are the workhorses of a healthy garden, and I had none.

It didn't bother me then. I don't like worms of any kind. They are too creepy, too crawly, and entirely too snaky.

But Matthan adores them. He trots along behind me when I'm digging or tilling, collecting earthworms until his hands are full of them and worms dangle, wiggling, from between his fingers. Sometimes he asks for a jar. "It's for my worms," he explains. "I want to keep my worms in it."

I still don't especially like worms. But I've learned to appreciate the earthworms that live in my gardens, and that's a good thing, because their numbers have increased to that of a vast army. As long as I don't have to see them, I even like to think about all of them living beneath the mulch and turning the soil into a wonderland of nutrients for my plants.

I'm continually amazed at the way all the beneficial bugs and worms contribute to the health of my garden, and I've learned to welcome them. But I will probably never gather them up in my hands to treasure them the way Matthan does.

The things in my life that don't turn out as I'd want them to—the derailed plans and all the disappointments—sometimes seem a lot like earthworms to me. I know God must have a reason for them, a very good reason that I don't understand just yet. Later, when I look back over my life, I might begin to see what God's plan was for the things that turned sour or the mistakes I hadn't planned on, those earthworms in my life that seem so distasteful right now.

Or I might not. God owes me no explanation other than the one he gives in today's Scripture reading, verses 8-9: "For my thoughts are not your thoughts, neither are your ways my ways, saith the LORD. For as the heavens are higher than the earth, so are my ways higher than your ways, and my thoughts than your thoughts."

Prayer

There are so many things I can't understand, Lord, but this I do know: you are in control, and you even use the earthworms of my life to make good things happen.

Reflection

What is one thing in my life now that I don't like but which might be an "earthworm"?

7

WINTER STORM

Exodus 20:18-21; 2 Corinthians 6:14-18

Matthan is at the age when storms are fearful things. Sometimes just a scattering of raindrops from gray clouds is enough to send him into a panic.

We built our home into the mountainside just beyond the end of the lane, and behind our house the hillside slopes steeply downward. Standing at the glass doors to the back deck when a strong wind is lashing through the treetops about ten or fifteen feet away strikes fear in Matthan's heart. There are times when he seeks shelter in the dark cavity behind the couch.

Most often, though, the arms of his family are his preferred method of comfort. At the first rumble of thunder or the first sweep of wind along the treetops, he runs to whomever is closest to be soothed and cuddled.

I am afraid of some storms too. Not necessarily of the tempests that blow through the hills with wild gales that set the treetops to dancing and bending, but the ones that sweep over my life with sudden fury. The ones that settle down upon me with thick, smothering clouds and ice my soul with their frigid winds.

I'm afraid of the storms that bring to my heart a season that feels like a perpetual winter.

My favorite words in these verses of Exodus 20 are found in verse 21: "Moses drew near unto the thick darkness where God was."

God is in the midst of the storm! In the thick darkness, to be exact. Why fear the heavy clouds that settle over us, when that is where God is? There is no storm he hasn't seen coming, and no conflict that ever takes him by surprise. God is never caught off guard by the unfolding events that leave me reeling in shock.

In some ways, Matthan is wise. When storms come, he runs to the arms of those he loves and trusts. We don't stop the wind or turn a spigot to stop the torrents of rain, but we do our best to calm him. We go with him through the storm and emerge together on the other side.

God does no less for those who turn to him when the storms of life rage. After all, he has promised, "And I will receive you. And will be a Father unto you, and ye shall be my sons and daughters" (2 Corinthians 6:17-18). He might not stop the winds, nor does he automatically make everything better, but he does walk with us through the storm.

And when the storm is subsiding and the gusts of wind are slackening, he is still with us. Still beside us. He didn't leave us during the bad days or the worst hours. Just as I would never leave Matthan when he's afraid.

Prayer

Some of life's storms are frightening to the extreme, God. Remind me again that you have promised to walk through all my storms with me.

Reflection

Is someone I know experiencing a storm? How could I help?

1

FROM SCARS
TO FERNS

Joel 2:21-32; Romans 11:33-36

An old logging trail snakes down over the steep hillside just behind our house. Years ago it was a long, gaping scar on the mountain; skidders lumbered up the path dragging trees the loggers had cut.

The treads of the unwieldy logging equipment cut into the rocks of the mountain, churning aside roots and soil to leave behind deep and sullen scars all the way into the valley. Skidders and bulldozers are no delicate machines, and evidence of their forays into the forest is both ugly and overwhelming. They come to cut and destroy, and then they leave, but the damage remains.

But the deep and muddy furrows did not stay an unpleasant sight. Land heals. Leaves blanketed the long gash in the sloping soil, rains cleansed and settled it. Nearby trees shaded it. Seeds began to grow.

The last time we went for a stroll to the valley—or what more closely resembled a headlong slide into the valley—we followed the old skidder trail down the mountain. It still snaked between the trees. More than twenty years later, we could still plainly see where the heavy equipment had maneuvered up and down the hill. It might take a lifetime or longer to erase all the evidence.

But it was no longer ugly. The little trail that dipped between two rolling heaps of shoved-aside soil was the prettiest place on the mountain. The leaves had settled deeply there, and ferns grew thick and green in the sheltered spots.

It was autumn as we crunched our way down through the leaves and ferns. When I lifted some roots from the moist soil to examine them, I was fascinated. Deep in the hard knob above the root was the tight whorl that would uncurl into the delicate fern fronds come spring.

All along the trail, the ferns were settling down to winter but holding within their hearts the promise of new growth and another spring.

Here God had restored "the years that the locust hath eaten" (Joel 2:25), and he had done so magnificently. The old logging trail, once torn by treads, damaged and ugly, was now an attractive part of the forest. In forgiving and healing, it had been granted an extra dose of loveliness.

Isn't that so often how God works in our lives? Even when we cannot see or understand until years afterward, we can rest assured that God knows what he is about to accomplish. He can heal our wounds and repair our scars and grant us the strength to forgive those who inflicted them in the first place. And from the rain and mud of damage and sorrow, the prettiest flowers of life often find moisture to grow.

Prayer

Please take the scars and the wounds and the ugly of my life, O Lord. Restore everything to bring honor and glory to you.

Reflection

Today I will take one step away from an old wound. How can I do this?

2

CODY'S FLOWER

Isaiah 64:4-12

I remember few bouquets as well as I remember the single clematis flower Cody brought me one day when he was about five. I had been admiring those flowers for days. The vines sprawled through a lilac bush, and fat buds were opening into lavender-striped flowers the size of soup plates. I couldn't seem to stop looking at them.

From the time they were just learning to toddle, the children have liked my flower gardens. Because I spent so much time there, they did too. I used to think—and still do—that there is no prettier picture in all the world than children absorbed in play among the flowers.

Of course, they also learned young to like picking flowers, and busy little fingers often gathered bouquets to bring indoors. From the first daffodils and grape hyacinths in spring to the last sprigs of chrysanthemums before frost, the children liked to keep the vases full.

So when Cody brought that single huge flower indoors, we floated it in a bowl of water. It was just as striking on the table as rambling over a bush.

Several hours later, I chanced to walk past that lilac bush, and I glanced at the clematis. It was habit. The flowers were just too lovely and too prolific to pass without a second or third glance. In fact, I often paused there, just to look at them.

But something was certainly wrong today. The huge flowers hung limp and faded; the leaves drooped. There was no purple splendor clinging to the lilac twigs.

I examined the clematis, wondering what form of blight could have struck it down in such a short time. It had been healthy just a few hours ago.

Close to the bottom of the stalk, I found the answer. The main vine had been severed. Everything above it was curled up and withering. The lower foliage was fine, but there were no flowers.

I could see so clearly what must have happened. Cody's little fingers grasping the bright flower nearest the base. The yanking and heaving to separate it from the vine. The smile on his face as he carried it lovingly indoors. And the dying vines he left behind.

How often, I wonder now, do I do the same to God? How often do I mean to bring him an offering, an act of service, and leave behind a trampled trail of stumbling footprints and hurting hearts? How often he must wish I had asked for guidance before I leaped headfirst into a predicament. Instead of waiting for his leading, I so often rush along, determined to have my way and to bring my offerings to God in my own time.

I still liked the flower floating in the bowl on the table. I loved the reason it was there, and that Cody had brought it to me. I think God looks as patiently and lovingly at each small thing I try to do for him. But I also think he wants me to slow down and look around. There is no reason to neglect or hurt people around me because I am busy serving God. It should be the other way around. When I serve those around me, then I am serving God.

Prayer

I need to remember, Lord, that there are many ways to do things for you. Quietly helping the people around me is more important to you than great deeds of some splendid service elsewhere.

Reflection

How can I serve God today by serving my family?

3

PROCRASTINATION

Acts 24:26

*W*hen writing is going well, there is almost no place I would rather be than seated at my desk. It just takes discipline to get there, and sometimes that is lacking.

Today was another of those times when I found myself delaying. Because writing is also hard work, and sometimes I would rather do almost anything else.

First I noticed the children's Simon game lying nearby, so I picked it up and played a few rounds. Then I remembered that I had wanted to find my jump rope. After all, writing involves a lot of sitting, and I wasn't getting much exercise these days. Time to crack down on my lazy habits.

I finally unearthed a jump rope. It was on the bottom of a plastic toy tub in the den, hidden by in-line skates, a football, and a red firefighter helmet the boys play with sometimes. I took my rope to the kitchen. I would use it there, sandwiching exercise between cooking and dishes and helping the children learn their Bible verses for memory class at school.

Next I noticed four pots of amaryllis on the windowsill beside the desk. They looked dry, so I fetched a glass of water and remedied that. The flowers seemed grateful, but I hadn't yet written a single word.

Dawdling at my desk, I recalled some classic cases of delay. Hadn't King Agrippa done the same thing several thousand years ago when he said to Paul, "Almost thou persuadest me to be a Christian" (Acts 26:28)?

King Agrippa was delaying too. Did he think about everything in his life that did not yet fall in line with Jesus' teachings? Did a full surrender look too hard? He might have thought he wanted to believe. Someday. Maybe tomorrow or the next day.

Governor Felix, as he listened to Paul's words, was certainly convicted. Yet he delayed too and sent Paul away, saying, "Go thy way for this time; when I have a convenient season [time], I will call for thee" (Acts 24:25).

The New Testament doesn't tell us whether these men ever stopped delaying and found a day that was convenient enough to accept the Savior and Lord about whom Paul was telling them. They had ample opportunity, but all we know for certain is that they chose to delay their decision. Usually when one delays long enough, the inclination disappears, so it seems probable that they never did find the right time to decide to open their hearts and accept God's offer of salvation. We do need a certain amount of discipline, a will that is surrendered to obedience, and a willingness to take time to absorb the things of God.

And yet, when I finally resist the strong urge to delay until a more convenient time, when I realize that *now* is the time to begin living in a way that is pleasing to God rather than to myself, then suddenly I'm ready.

Every beginning, every small step toward God, opens the way for the next one.

And then there is no place I would rather be. No delay among the mundane of in-line skates or jump ropes or plants is important enough to detain me when God calls.

The time to serve him is certainly now. The time to answer him is now. And the time to work is now.

Prayer

Lord, when it seems you are asking much of me, may I remember that you gave your life for me. Nothing is too much for me to surrender to you.

Reflection

How am I delaying when it comes to committing myself more fully to God?

4

CHILDREN AND DOCTORS

Isaiah 61; Matthew 9:10-13;
Mark 2:15-17; Luke 5:29-32

*J*t was one of those days again, and I guess every mom has them—the days when it seems we should have had nurse's training before becoming a mother.

Matthan woke with a hoarse whoop and a croak, as is so typical of him when he is starting a cold. I gave him a nebulizer treatment immediately to make him more comfortable.

Alisha did not get up at all. She said her stomach hurt, and later she had a fever. She had obviously caught the flu that was going around.

And that afternoon, Cody came home from school in a rush with blood dripping from his nose. He's prone to nosebleeds every winter, and this one was fairly bad. I scurried around trying to remember how to doctor a nosebleed like this one. Cold cloth to the back of his neck. Pinch lightly on the bridge of his nose. Sit forward instead of leaning back. Should I be remembering anything else?

The next day I took Matthan to the doctor. He wasn't that sick, but I had used the last of the albuterol for his treatments the previous night, and he needed to be seen before Dr. Marsha would prescribe more. It was as much to make me comfortable, because I was worried he would need another treatment, and I didn't want to be without the medicine.

I appreciated the doctor's gentle manner and her obvious knowledge about all things medical, but especially about little boys whose airways become tight and who find it hard to breathe as soon as a bad cold comes along.

Because I have little or no gift of nursing, I am extremely grateful for the doctors who bring relief to my children when they need it. In such doctors one can catch glimpses of the way God cares for us—his beloved children. We all need a soul doctor in one way or another.

"They that are whole [healthy]," Jesus tells us, "have no need of the physician, but they that are sick: I came not to call the righteous, but sinners to repentance" (Mark 2:17).

Jesus wants to heal our heartaches, forgive our sins and stumbles, bandage our errors and missteps. He is the ultimate doctor for all. He has been sent "to bind up the brokenhearted" (Isaiah 61:1). In addition to healing broken bodies, Jesus is also skilled at healing broken hearts. No case is too hard for him to handle, and he knows our individual needs. He knows what we need better than we do. Why not give him all the sorrows and sicknesses of our souls? He can make us whole in surprising ways.

Prayer

Bring healing to all the splintered and hurting places in my heart, Lord. You are the only one who can know exactly what I need to make me whole in body and spirit.

Reflection

Is there anyone close to me who needs comfort and healing today? How can I help?

5

YOUR SPEECH
BETRAYS YOU

Matthew 26:56-75; Luke 6:43-45

*M*y husband, Laverne, has a woodworking and finishing shop at home, and he meets many new people each year. Some come once or twice and are soon forgotten. Others come once or twice and are long remembered.

Such was the case of a man who came one day a number of years ago. He had made a few small rocking chairs and he wanted them stained and varnished. It was something Laverne was glad to do for him, and they discussed colors, stains, prices, and how soon Laverne could have them finished.

"That new customer must be a Christian," Laverne remarked later after the man had gone. "He was such a nice, decent fellow, and his language was so clean. It was a pleasure to do business with him."

Not long afterward, we found out that he was indeed a member of a Christian church, but we weren't surprised. He had already told us so, almost without using any words at all. We could have said of him what was said to Peter so long ago: "Surely thou also art one of them, for thy speech bewrayeth [betrays] thee" (Matthew 26:73).

That day in the shop, our new customer plainly showed us who the King of his life was. His decent language, clothes, and manner told us whom he was serving.

When I wear plain clothes and show my affiliation to a certain church, then people also have certain expectations of me. For instance, they expect me to act in a way that clearly shows Christ is the King I am serving.

All my plain clothes won't mean a thing if I then turn around and act in a way that is not Christlike. I can dress modestly and still spread gossip and disunity among family and friends. I can harbor bitterness, envy, greed, anger, and more in the heart that beats beneath my plain cape dress. If I do, my speech and actions will soon reveal whom I serve, even if I'm dressed conservatively.

If Jesus is the ruler of my life, it must begin in my heart and then spread outward to touch every area of my life. A modest and conservative way of dress should be a sign of a vibrant faith that is alive and well. All my words and actions should correspond with the faith I call my own.

And it should become such a big part of who I am that everyone I meet will know Jesus is the one I follow.

Even if I don't use any words at all to tell them.

Prayer

Lord, let every area of my life show that I serve you. Open my eyes to the places that still need improvement.

Reflection

What is one thing I can change in my life today that will show I am serious about the One whom I serve?

6

STICKING OUT

2 Corinthians 5:17-21

A story is told about a small boy who waited to speak to the minister of a church after the services were over. He understood that he was a sinner, and he wondered what he should do in order to become a Christian.

The minister spent some time with that boy. He explained how it was necessary for him to repent of his sins and to ask Jesus for help to forsake them. "You have to invite Jesus to come and live in your heart," the minister said.

The young boy was startled. "Oh no, sir, I couldn't do that," he exclaimed. "I'm so small and Jesus is so big. He would be sticking out all over."

"He would, indeed," came the minister's reply. "That's the whole point of inviting him in, young man."

Amid my daily life—cleaning children, windows, bathrooms, and floors; cooking scores of meals each year; hanging laundry and making sure the pets are fed—I quite frequently forget that I'm to have Jesus "sticking out all over." I start complaining instead. I whine about cooking or gripe about the weather. In fact, if I really put my mind to it, it's surprising how many things I can find to grumble about.

Other times, I'm downright rude. I don't intend to be, but in my rush to do my duties, I forget to be considerate. I don't take seriously enough the "Do as you would be done to" rule for living, and I begin to act as if it were instead an optional and possibly obsolete text from ancient years.

Living with Jesus sticking out all over must become a way of life. If his spirit permeates every corner of my heart, it's going to show to those around me. For it must begin at home and extend from there in a shining circle.

Doing the ordinary tasks of my life as if I were doing them for Jesus removes them from the mundane and renders them worthwhile. And it will make me able to reach out to others in a way that gives clear evidence of who is running my life.

Instead of complaining, I should praise God for all he has done for me. And if I put my mind to it, that list never really ends. Instead of rushing around rude and grouchy, I will slow down and acknowledge that I am one of the "ambassadors for Christ" (2 Corinthians 5:20).

I will begin to let him stick out all over.

Prayer

I wish everyone I meet could see that you are living in me, Lord. Continue to show me how to bring honor to your name.

Reflection

How will I be an ambassador for Christ today?

7

SMALL BEGINNINGS

Matthew 25:14-29

*W*hen I was asked to begin working on what would possibly become this devotional book, I felt some sneaking sympathy for the servant who buried his talent. The task looked too large. It would be far easier to decline the offer.

The parable of the master with the three servants and the talents he gave them always makes me wonder. There are so many questions. For instance, why did the servant who buried his talent think that was the easiest route? Was it indolence, or something more complicated? And the faithful servants who worked hard and doubled their talents: How did they feel the first day after their master left? Eager to begin proving they were capable of this task? Or overwhelmed by the responsibility that was now theirs?

We aren't told how long the master was gone on his journey. But if he was traveling into a far country, it's probably safe to assume he was gone for quite a few years.

I imagine the faithful servants didn't significantly increase their master's goods the first day. Likely not even the first month. But I believe daily they worked faithfully at that which needed to be done that day. No doubt it took a long time and a lot of work to turn five talents into ten. It took just as long and just as much work to change two into four. Yet the amount they started with and the amount they ended with was not as important as what they did with it.

When their master returned, he was pleased for two reasons. They had been willing to work with what he had given them, and they faithfully took care of it for him to claim when he returned.

The servant who was so harshly denounced and stripped of all he had was the one who refused to use even that small bit which he had. Did he ever begin? Did he start but find the work hard, and give up because it wasn't easy? How did he spend that long time while his master was gone? Was it in idleness, wickedness, or merely self-indulgence? The only thing we really know is that he gave up. He had nothing to show for his efforts when the master returned.

When faced with a daunting task, I remember this man. If the work is great and I can make only a small beginning, even that is better than not doing anything at all. Tomorrow I will add a little more to that. And the next day a bit more. And the next day . . .

Prayer

When the load appears too large for me, Lord, remind me to focus on one small step first. And remind me too that you are beside me to help carry the burden you've laid upon me.

Reflection

What small beginning to some large task can I make today?

1

CHOCOLATE AND STORIES

Psalm 103

It was late afternoon on Christmas Eve, and I was wrapping up the last-minute details on the treats I needed to bring to the family dinner at my parents' house the next day. Date balls and Rice Krispies squares were ready and wrapped. Cookies were cooling, and I was melting chocolate to spread over the top. In a few minutes, I would be done.

Or so I thought. When I removed the top of the double boiler, I accidentally let drops of moisture slide into the chocolate, so much so that the chocolate seized and turned into a hard lump while I stirred. There was no way to use it, and I scraped it out and started over.

While the second batch melted, I left it to do a few other jobs that were waiting. Alas, I tarried too long and the second batch burned. It was charred and gritty and tasted terrible. I scraped it out too.

By now the children were concerned. They feared I would ask them to eat cookies without a chocolate glaze, and that would be dreadful, they thought. I was both concerned and immensely aggravated at myself. Why couldn't I be better at cooking?

Alisha and I hung breathlessly over the third batch of chocolate as it melted, and at last we spread it, smooth and glossy, over the cookies. They looked perfect now, with a sprinkling of chopped peanuts over top.

And as I worked with the third batch of chocolate, my irritation faded. I decided I would turn this annoying situation into a story, after which point it didn't seem quite so awful after all.

That story, "On Chocolate and Lessons," was published exactly a year later by *Written on My Heart* magazine. It paid enough to cover the cost of the chocolate I had burned, with some left over. By then I could laugh about it. Why had I let myself become so frustrated?

But isn't that how God works? He takes our well-meaning fumbling, our blunders and goofs and embarrassing mishaps, and turns them into something he can use. After all, he knows how fearfully human we are. "For he knoweth our frame; he remembereth that we are dust" (Psalm 103:14).

The unintentional mistakes, the times I really messed up, the willful sins repented of—God can use them all. It is he "who redeemeth thy life from destruction" (verse 4). He wants to help save us from the ways we mess up, ways that are much more serious than burned chocolate.

So he is working to bring good out of all things (Romans 8:28). When we at last surrender our stubborn selfishness, our pride, our stiff-necked attitudes, then he can come into our hearts and lives and work miracles we wouldn't have thought possible. But first we must grant him entrance.

If I can find a way to redeem carelessly burned chocolate, how much more will God be able to make good come even from the things in my life that look wrong or hopeless?

Prayer

Lord, I give my whole life into your hands, and that includes the problems I've made, and the ways I've messed up. May you find a way to use it all for your glory.

Reflection

When I look back over my life today, what is one thing I thought was a mistake at the time but that God used for good instead?

2

DIFFERENCES

Romans 3:9-31

I wake up most mornings ready to dive into my day. I like to have my hours organized and well begun by eight or earlier. But by evening I've started to fade, and my energy levels are depleted.

Laverne wakes up more slowly. If he has a large job to tackle, he would rather work late into the night to finish it. He's usually still going strong at suppertime and ready to put in several more hours in the shop.

I don't really like to cook. Food seems to have a mind of its own, and recipes seldom turn out as I expected. I have cooked up some most interesting glops that no one wants to eat.

My mother-in-law loves to cook. She just really likes feeding people. Twenty for lunch does not faze her, nor that many more for supper. Ingredients obey her command and turn into marvelous dishes.

I can never have too many books, and I consider it a fruitful year when I have purchased dozens more to add to my shelves. If I have a book to read and time to read it, I am usually perfectly happy.

Not so for one of my friends. For her, books are a nuisance at best, and depressing at worst. Being forced to sit alone and read a lot would be a punishment to her rather than a source of joy.

Author Jean Hersey has written, "There is but one mountain we are all climbing, but many, many paths up it, and we are each drawn to the path that is right for us."[1]

God has created the most amazing diversity in his universe. But in people, his crowning glory, the differences are mind-boggling. How can there be billions of people, yet not one of them is the same?

One might think that children born to the same parents and who grow up in the same home under the same circumstances with the same rules would be more similar to each other. Yet each arrives as a perfect little package of new humanity with a personality all his or her own, and each child develops into an amazingly distinct new person.

Sometimes I forget to consider this. I forget that not everyone thinks as I do (and nor would I want them to). Instead of fretting about this, I should celebrate the differences in everyone around me.

Yet despite all our differences, some things are the same for each one of us. Every person—created by God and shaped by his or her past, surroundings, circumstances—is on the same journey up this mountain of life. We all "have sinned, and come short of the glory of God" (Romans 3:23). Yet Jesus has died for every single one of us, and every person on the globe has a decision to make accordingly: to accept that gift or reject it.

And each one of us must discover our own path. We must each climb our own mountain and find our own way to God. Perhaps our differences are only on the surface. Underneath it all, we are more alike than we sometimes realize.

Prayer

Lord, teach me how to celebrate the different personalities of the people around me, even while I remember that for all of us, one thing is the same: your love for each soul.

Reflection

In what ways am I different from the people around me? How are we similar?

3

CONTENTMENT AND BASEBALL BATS

Luke 12:15; 1 Timothy 6:6-19

I was cleaning the basement at our two-room parochial school when the door banged open. With a great deal of effort, two young neighbor children were hauling armloads of baseball bats in from the playground.

"What a lot of bats," I said above the noise of about a dozen, give or take, clanging into a box.

"Yes, and the boys want still more!" Evelyn exclaimed.

Why was I not surprised? Perhaps because one of the boys in grade 8 was my son, and I'd heard his opinion of why a certain bat, of a certain brand, would do so much to improve their game.

Or maybe it was because I knew how the-more-you-get-the-more-you-want syndrome worked. After all, I'd encountered it often enough in my own life. Not about bats, you may be sure, but about other things.

I wondered again why this should be so. Why do I still sometimes think I need one more thing to be truly satisfied? Why is it that no matter how much you have, something is still lacking? Why does anyone still think more wealth or more possessions of some sort would satisfy that internal restlessness?

It must be that we seek contentment in things while forgetting that contentment is inside us. People were created for worship, and instead of worshiping the God who can truly satisfy our longings, we often worship things. Things as temporal and handcrafted as the wood and stone idols of long ago.

No doubt we've all seen what can happen when things are given too much space in our lives. Those who spend their years in relentless pursuit of earthly treasures, always building bigger and ever seeking more, become unhappier all the while. They have an empty sort of life. There's always one more baseball bat they don't have.

At last I begin to understand that contentment is like joy, and "joy is not in things, it is in us," as pastor and writer Charles Wagner has written.[2] But it is also something that must be learned. Paul the apostle says, "For I have learned, in whatsoever state I am, therewith to be content" (Philippians 4:11). Two verses later, he adds, "I can do all things through Christ which strengtheneth me."

Notice that Paul doesn't say, "I was born knowing how to be content in all things." Rather, he says, "I have learned." Is it too much to suppose that every one of us must learn contentment for ourselves too?

And when Paul adds, "I can do all things through Christ," he minces no words. For Christ is the answer to all our longings, all our dissatisfied feelings. More baseball bats (of whatever sort) won't make anyone any happier for any length of time.

But the joy of the risen Christ poured into our seeking hearts— that will bring lasting contentment and peace.

Prayer

The glitter and the glamour of things are so alluring, Lord. I have to be reminded again and again that only the things of eternal value truly satisfy.

Reflection

Today, I resolve to stop seeking my happiness in things. How will I do this?

4

WINTER HOMECOMING

Matthew 5:1-12; Hebrews 10:34-39

*I*n winter, it gets dark early here in the hills, and by late afternoon the lights are shining through the gathering darkness. Supper is on the stove and everyone will soon come inside.

The children are home from school or work. Laverne puts aside his labor, closes the shop door, and walks to the house. In the dark, through the rain or snow or violet gloom of a winter evening, a yellow glow of light shimmers in each window. It promises many things to those of us who will simply open the front door and walk on in.

Through that door is our home, a haven from the darkness of the winter night outside. A wood fire is keeping the house warm, lamplight makes everything cozy, and the wavering flame of a scented candle adds a cheery note. Good smells lace the air: spaghetti bubbles on the stove, the children's favorite biscuits cool on the counter, muffins pebbled with blueberries are ready to be removed from the oven. The rooms are alive with all the sounds of family gathered near.

I am a homemaker, and I love making a home for my family. Best of all, I love when they all come home again after a busy day away from me. There are few things as dear to my heart as a winter evening around the table with the cold world shut outside.

God is a homemaker too. He has created a home for those who love and serve him, for all those who obey his commandments. He's called it heaven, and he's there now. Perhaps he is putting the finishing touches on the meal he has prepared, and is moving toward the door. I believe he's eager to welcome inside every person who has accepted Jesus as Savior, who has truly repented of and forsaken sin, and who is following the way of the cross. Those are the members of the family he will be inviting home any time now.

It will be a homecoming like none we've experienced yet. "Eye hath not seen, nor ear heard, neither have entered into the heart of man, the things which God hath prepared for them that love him" (1 Corinthians 2:9). Inside that golden front door is a love and a splendor our eyes and ears and hearts are too small and weak and earthbound to comprehend.

"The LORD's throne is in heaven" (Psalm 11:4), and it is there where his saints will worship him forever. Life on earth is a lot like the cold harshness of winter sometimes, but life on earth is only a small part of the story. Beyond this winter there is a homecoming so alive with radiance, a home so full of love, that we have no way to imagine what it will be like.

Prayer

O God, prepare me for the home you have created. Clean my heart of anything that would prevent me from entering that front door of heaven.

Reflection

What more should I be doing today to prepare for heaven?

5

WHAT TIME
I AM AFRAID

Psalm 56

*M*atthan is four years old, and his world is widening rapidly. He has so many questions and so many fears.

The things he's afraid of don't always make sense to me. A small plastic beaver with its mouth open, showing long teeth ready to gnaw off trees, instills a great fear in him. So he throws the beaver into a drawer and slams it shut. But even with the beaver out of sight, Matthan is worried.

"I can hear him racketing around in there, Mom," he tells me. And even when I assure him I can't and that he's perfectly safe where a plastic toy animal is concerned, he's not so sure.

I have fears too, and they seem more reasonable than Matthan's. I worry about war, persecution, insecticides, and poverty, to name a few. I worry even more about the kind of world in which my children are growing up, about the rampant evil that seems to be gaining an upper hand everywhere.

Perhaps my fears make more sense to God than Matthan's do to me. Or perhaps they do not. After all, God has promised to take care of those who trust in his name and to keep us in the shelter of his hand. So he didn't promise me an easy way with no concerns, but he did promise to walk it with me. He expects me to trust that he knows what is going on, that he sees the big picture, even when I don't.

Sometimes I can explain away Matthan's fears. When he understands that the things he's worried about are normal or are nothing to fear, he believes me. The look of concern fades from his face. He might still not be able to see his worries as I see them, but he trusts me.

I say I trust God. Bad things do happen, but I say I believe God knows what he's doing and that he is in control. So if I say I trust him, I should let my worries fade, my anxieties be subdued. I don't always know what's going on. But God does. I can learn to say with the psalmist in verse 3 of today's Scripture, "What time I am afraid, I will trust in thee."

Prayer

Lord, I know you love me as much as I love my children. You care when I'm worried or concerned about something, and I know you will help me if I ask.

Reflection

How can I be less fearful and more trusting today?

6

THE RESULTS OF PAIN

Psalm 25

Sometimes pain is how God gets our attention. When we're hurt, he can teach us more than he can when we're happy.

When I wonder about that, I notice how it works for my children. A pinched finger hurts, and they remember to be more careful next time. Something like a bee sting really gets their attention. Not only do they make wide detours around places where bees and wasps might lurk, but they also learn empathy through the deal. When a sibling or friend is stung, they know the experience is painful, and they can sympathize. Misbehavior that brings certain and unpleasant consequences will not be so readily repeated. Pain is God's megaphone, observed C. S. Lewis: "God whispers to us in our pleasures, speaks in our conscience, but shouts in our pain: it is His megaphone to rouse a deaf world."[3]

Verse 18 of today's Scripture is a plea to God to remember us when we're hurting: "Look upon mine affliction and my pain."

When life hurts, we want God to remember us. We want some acknowledgment that he sees what we're going through. But mostly we want him to notice our pain and take it away. We want him to remove the mountains we don't want to climb, those mountains that hurt our feet so much. Yet often it is only when we climb those mountains that we can look back down into the valley and see what we learned in the wearying climb.

So pain serves a great purpose in God's plan for my life. I don't always like it, but when I remember to look deeper to find what it might be teaching me, I am occasionally surprised. Even in a pleasant way.

If pain is the way God gets my attention, I accept it. Not always willingly, it is true, but a measure of acceptance brings a measure of peace.

Isaiah 24:15 goes still one step further. The prophet says, "Glorify ye the LORD in the fires."

The only way to do this, I find, is by believing the fires, or trials, in my life are for a reason. Perhaps only God really understands that reason now, but if I accept it patiently—and maybe even if I don't—he will use the bad to teach me many necessary things I would not learn otherwise. And God will comfort me through the grief and difficult times.

Prayer

Lord, when the fires come into my life, I will try to praise you anyway. Even when I can't understand the reason or see the results, peace comes when I trust that you know what is happening and why it must be.

Reflection

What is one good thing I have learned from pain?

7

CORINTHIANS TODAY

Acts 18:1-17; Philippians 2:12-16

*I*n the apostle Paul's day, Corinth was the most famous and influential city in Greece. It was a teeming hub of national business, idol-worshiping religion, and debased refinement.

In the midst of this degraded city, Paul established a church. Acts 18:1-17 describes his struggles to achieve this. Two of his letters are written to "the church of God which is at Corinth" (1 Corinthians 1:2; 2 Corinthians 1:1). In these books of the New Testament, Paul devotes many verses to the problems and conflicts that resulted when this heathen society encountered the message of Jesus Christ as the risen Lord.

But in this pagan culture, and among those who did not acknowledge the God of creation, a fledgling church was started. Both 1 and 2 Corinthians are Paul's letters to the believers there, and they focus on the many problems that concerned both individuals and the church. Poor Paul must have been frustrated many times by these people and their lack of faith.

What if the apostle Paul should come to my country today? Would he see some striking similarities between my nation and the ancient Corinthians of Greece?

In every generation and among every society, the disciples of Jesus have encountered temptations and trials unique to their time and place. If you plan to serve God, he will want to see if you are sincere about it. There will be tests to pass. And sometimes the amount of effort you make, the things you surrender in order to follow Christ, and the attitude with which you do it will be the most important tests of all.

Whether one was a Christian in Paul's newly established church at Corinth two thousand years ago or a Christian in North America today, in which atheistic and agnostic thought involves a fast-increasing segment of our society, or a Christian in any era in between, our work is the same. Philippians 2:15 explains clearly God's desire for all those who call themselves his followers: "That ye may be blameless and harmless, the sons of God, without rebuke, in the midst of a crooked and perverse nation, among whom ye shine as lights in the world."

Prayer

I need your help, Lord, to shine with your love and grace and peace. May all those I meet today be able to see that you are living in my heart.

Reflection

What is one way I could shine as a child of God today?

1

THIS IS FAITH

Mark 11:22-33

I awoke this morning to gray skies sagging with clouds. It rained for a while, but as the temperatures dropped, the rain changed to snow. The flakes fell furiously from the sky, driven before a rising wind that grew colder as the day drew toward evening.

Even at noon the day had an appearance of dusk. Yet I knew the sun was still there, following its daily course across the sky. I didn't doubt this for an instant. I couldn't see it, but I knew it was there, shining behind the clouds.

I have never seen God nor spoken face-to-face with the Creator of the universe. But I know he's there. I don't doubt this for an instant. I feel his presence in the sunshine and in the hugs of those I love. I see it in the majesty of the rolling hills, in the delicacy of a dainty flower. I hear it in the laughter of a child and the call of a bird.

But there are dark days in life too. Weeks when the gray clouds of heartache seem to suffocate even the breath of life. There are hours bleak with worry and fear and sorrow, and they come to every life. As soon as an infant draws that first breath, he or she is subject to pain. I've never met anyone who was exempt from gray clouds, both in weather and in life.

Today I have a choice. I can look out at the clouds and decide that's all there is. Or I can look at the clouds and remember that the sun is shining just behind them. Either way, the clouds are there.

When I'm feeling the gray of heartache all through my soul, I have a choice too. I can focus on the clouds until I see nothing else and thereby become bitter and angry. At God and at those around me.

Or I can believe the clouds are there for a reason. That God, who guides even the clouds, knows what this time of heartache is supposed to accomplish in my life.

And this is faith. Not the absence of clouds or sorrows, but the choice to believe in the sunshine, in the goodness of God, even when we can't see or feel it.

I believe the sun will shine again, even if it's cloudy this week. I believe in God, even in the dark times when it seems he isn't near.

Prayer

Lord, when the skies are dark, help me to remember that you are still beside me. I can't see you, but that doesn't mean you aren't here.

Reflection

What are the clouds in my life today, and how might God be using them to help me?

2

DECISIONS

Galatians 5:13-26

*M*any chapters in the New Testament are a call to obedience to Christ. Notice that it is a call, an invitation. God doesn't force anyone into obedience. He never makes any of us follow Christ if we insist on our own will instead of his. He invites us to come, to share eternity with him, but he doesn't make us come. He gives every person that freedom of choice.

So I get to choose. I choose the kind of life I want to live, and by doing so, I also choose my destiny. How many people today are choosing their eternal destiny by making no decision at all?

Yet even to drift aimlessly is our decision to make.

Our Scripture reading for today lists the works of the flesh and, immediately afterward, the fruit of the Spirit produced when one has decided to heed God's call. It's up to each individual to choose one or the other. To open one's heart to the Holy Spirit or to the darker spirits that do not come from God.

To be like Christ is the true definition of the word *Christian*.

If I call myself a Christian, I also better be making decisions that are like those Christ would make.

When someone uses me unkindly, steals from me, speaks all manner of evil and slander about me and mine, then I decide how I will react. There's that crucial first moment—will I become angry and speak bitter accusations in return? Or will I choose to be like Christ? Will I decide in favor of love, forgiveness, graciousness?

When I feel I have reason to hate, I can decide to love instead by asking God to love through me. When my own strength is small, or even gone completely, I can decide to lean on the divine strength of Christ.

I can choose prayer rather than whining, and positive thoughts rather than negative ones. I can choose to focus on what God has done for me rather than on what he hasn't.

There are so many things in life that are beyond my control, so many situations I wish I could change, but it's impossible to do so. Then I have to decide—how will I respond to this? With anger and bitterness? With acceptance, submission, and then peace?

What about the times I forget and respond in a way that is less than Christlike? Even then I can still decide between good and bad. I can return and make amends, apologize, ask forgiveness. That is deciding to be more like Christ.

Every one of us makes scores, even hundreds, of decisions a day. If we fervently desire to be a Christian, our choices must reflect that desire.

And all our decisions at last decide our soul's destiny. There is no other way around it.

Prayer

Please help me to focus on the decision I've made to serve you, and you alone, O Lord. May all the other decisions I make in life correspond with this choice.

Reflection

What are some choices I could make today to show that I am a Christian?

3

FALLS OF LIFE

Acts 27

*I*n his wonderful book *When God Doesn't Make Sense*, James Dobson tells the story of a man who was on an eight-day trip downriver with some friends and the raft master who was guiding their raft. They encountered some treacherous rapids during their journey, but none as bad as the day they dropped over some falls in a canyon where the river sank thirty-seven vertical feet in a distance of seventy-five.

There, in the icy spray, with the roar of the churning water thundering in their ears, the raft master seemed to lose control, and their raft was flung sideways in the rapids. It was a terrible moment.

The man considered jumping: to leap from the raft and pit his strength against that of the frenzied river as it poured downward through the rapids. Fleetingly, that seemed to be a choice preferable to perishing with the floundering raft.

But he held on, and as he looked back, he could see what had happened. The raft master had spun the craft sideways on purpose. He did so to steer past an immense jagged rock that had fallen into the river from the canyon walls far above them. By going sideways hard and fast, he used the full power of the motor to push them safely past the jutting rock.

Now the man could see that if he had jumped into the river, he would certainly have died. Leaving the safety of the boat would have killed him instantly. It only appeared that the raft master had lost control of the situation. In reality, he was guiding the craft with great expertise. The raft was sideways for a reason, and the guide knew exactly what he was doing. Those in the boat were safe as long as they stayed with him.

In Dobson's book, he quotes the words of his friend Bob Vernon: "To those of you who are plunging over the falls today, resist the temptation to jump overboard! God knows what He is doing. He has your raft sideways for a reason."[4]

Has your raft ever been flung sideways in the spray? Does nothing make sense anymore? That has happened to me on occasion. Haven't we all at one time or another experienced that sinking feeling of seeing our secure life spiraling out of control?

That's when we make a most important decision. Sometimes it's a split-second reaction. Other times it's a dogged determination to hold on, a determination that must be renewed daily.

Will we believe the Raft Master of life has lost control, and jump into the rapids swirling around us? Or will we trust that God knows what he is doing, and honor our commitment to follow him?

In verse 31 of our Scripture for today, Paul tells us what to do: "Except these abide in the ship, ye cannot be saved."

Take Paul's words to heart: "If you don't stay on the boat, you won't make it to shore." Or reword it like this: "If you turn away from God, he cannot take you safely through the falls and rapids in your life."

Prayer

Lord, there are many things in life that I don't understand. Help me remember that you know all things and that you will give me the strength to keep my commitment to you, even when things don't make sense.

Reflection

How can I remain committed to God today?

4

JUMPING SHIP

John 21

In the previous devotional, we explored James Dobson's story of an adventure on a real white-water river trip. Not so long ago, my congregation experienced a figurative white-water trip that could point to lessons learned in the sideways lunge of the "craft" in which we rode. The distant mutter of the rapids became a full-throated roar as the "river" plunged us and our boat straight through the "falls."

I think I had been riding in one of the backseats, almost as if I were near the end of the boat. And I was enjoying the ride. It was a pleasant journey through scenic countryside. I had my faith, my family, a church full of friends. God seemed to be smiling, and I thanked him every day.

Then the canyon walls loomed dark and forbidding, the rapids swirled with deadly force, and cold spray drenched all of us in the boat. This was also part of the ride of life, but it was one I hadn't counted on, and God wasn't explaining why he had taken us this long way around.

It was a dark time, a dangerous time. Would we trust the pilot of our boat to steer us safely around the jagged rocks that thrust above the foaming waters? Would we lose confidence in the One who had brought us this way, and jump ship? Was it safer in the whirlpools around us or in the boat that might at any moment be dashed against the rocks?

It was natural to fear the tempest, to cringe from the cold spray, and to long for the safety and security of earlier days. But jumping from the ship could not be the answer either.

In *When God Doesn't Make Sense*, Dobson addresses such situations by asking, "Have you considered jumping into the river and trying to swim to safety on your own? That is precisely what Satan would have you do. He wants you to give up on God, who seems to have lost control of your circumstances. But I urge you not to leave the safety of His protection. The Captain knows what He is doing."[5]

Yes, the Captain knows what he is doing. Why would we doubt that the outcome of every crisis is in his hands? If I jump from the ship, it's an indication that I'm giving up, when what I really should be doing is crouching down, taking a firmer grip, and holding more tightly to the promises of the Captain. He knows the way out of this. I don't.

In every lifetime, we encounter hours when it appears as if the raft is spinning out of control. Days when we can't see the sun for the fury of the storm. Nights when the stars seem forever gone behind the canopy of black clouds. As long as we're alive, there's always a chance our boat will be hurled sideways. The most important thing, in the midst of rapids we can't understand and maybe never will, is to not lose faith in the Captain.

He knows what he is doing. If I hold on to him, I don't have to know.

Prayer

In the fury of the storm, O God, my faith is so small. But it is large enough to believe you are bigger than every storm.

Reflection

How can I, even in life's storms, hold fast to the things that matter?

5

DANGEROUS POWERS

Romans 8:38-39; Ephesians 6:10-20

The week I began outlining ideas for this book and tried to settle down to a reasonable writing schedule, I ran into all kinds of problems. Nothing wanted to work out.

On Monday I sat down on the recliner and dozed off. I didn't go near my desk. On Tuesday I was still tired. I went to spend the day with my mom and sisters, and I yawned a lot.

On Wednesday it was time to get serious about my work. I needed the familiar discipline of sitting down and picking up a pen.

Yet I continued to struggle through my writing hours over the next days. A bit of a struggle is nothing new, of course. Some days, words troop obediently along and paragraphs roll out as if oiled. Other days, finding words seems a bit like pulling teeth. There's a lot of groaning and yanking, but not much is happening.

But this didn't seem like a normal writer's issue, either. A sort of smothering, gloomy cloud had settled on me, and I couldn't seem to make any headway. I spent a lot of time holding my pen, shifting around in my chair, and staring at the wood grain on my desk.

It occurred to me, as I wrestled over and over with my uncooperative thoughts, that I would really like to give up. It was tempting to throw up my hands, call my editor, and say I couldn't do it. Only the memory of the contract I had signed prevented me from phoning.

On Saturday, in desperation, I called my friend in California who was working on the first book in this series. She listened to my sad tale and shared her own. On the days before her designated hours for working on her devotionals, she would feel the same way. "I have this feeling that I'm unable to do it. I get discouraged. I've begun to believe this is coming from Satan," she continued. "Think about it. He doesn't want us to write words to bring honor to God, and his power is very real. We'll have to pray harder and pray more. God can help us do this."

It was as if a light had suddenly flashed through the smothering cloud that was dragging me down. Somehow, I knew she was right, and with that knowledge came release from despair. I didn't like to think about the powers of darkness hovering over my desk, but at least I knew they were no match for the power of God. He is faithful to that which he has promised, and he has promised to be near all those who call on his name in truth (Psalm 145:18).

He would hear me when I prayed, and I knew how to pray. I could work once more. It was never exactly easy, this writing, but that terrible weight of hopelessness did not come again.

There's a reason life is often called a battlefield. The ongoing battle between good and evil reaches each one of us, and so do the consequences of our choices.

The powers of Satan can be overwhelming, and they are very real. His version warps everything God has designed to be good. Yet when we make a conscious decision to walk closer to God, when we desire above all else to live within his will and make every effort to do so, then Satan's power is bound. God's power in us can enable us to stand for what is good and right.

Prayer

Open my eyes, O God, and make me wise enough to see the snares the enemy of my soul spreads before me. Pick me up when I stumble, and help me to be willing to renounce all works that belong to Satan.

Reflection

What is one thing I could do today to show that God's power is the one that's ruling my life?

6

A NEW JERUSALEM

Revelation 3:7-13; 21

Could we get to Jerusalem from Grandma's house?" Matthan and I were on the way to Grandma's house for the day when he interrupted my thoughts with his surprising question.

"Uh, yes," I answered. "Yes, you could get to Jerusalem from there if you took the right roads." My mind was already speeding along the highways, a right turn here, a left there, and eventually one could arrive, I suppose, in Jerusalem. Getting there would just be a matter of knowing which roads to take, and perhaps shipping a car over waters when necessary.

I will probably never decide to travel to Jerusalem, so I didn't need to be concerned about the way to get there. But what about the New Jerusalem we read about in Revelation 3:12, where it says, "I will write upon him the name of my God, and the name of the city of my God, which is new Jerusalem"?

Now that was a place I didn't want to miss seeing. So how was I to get to the New Jerusalem? What road would take me there?

When Matthan asked whether we could get to Jerusalem from Grandma's house, the answer was yes. But first I had to know from where I was starting before I could decide the correct road to travel. In the same way, a desire to arrive someday at the gates of the New Jerusalem must begin inside each individual, and first we have to know where we are.

Is my heart full of bitterness or grudges or envy? Does sin have more of a hold on me than God does? Am I devoted to learning more about the things of God—or am I addicted to things that are harmful? What must be my first step on the road to the New Jerusalem?

It takes that willing first step, and then it takes a second one. It takes choosing the right turns, and the right roads, over and over. Sometimes it will be necessary to backtrack, to start over, to reroute and begin again. Because have you ever known anyone—anyone at all—who ended up on the correct road just by accident? Perhaps, but not very likely.

Taking the narrow, less traveled road that leads to the New Jerusalem involves deliberate thought as well as taking responsibility for our actions. I don't think anyone is going to drift aimlessly through that gate and say in surprise, "Why, how did I end up here?"

Rather, it will be a result of God's grace and Jesus' death on the cross, combined with my daily choices, my daily labor. Each day I must decide where I stand. Can I get to the New Jerusalem from here? Am I on the road that leads in the direction of that holy city?

And if the answer is no, if I've taken steps down a wide bypass or an alley that wanders to nowhere, I had better turn around and head back toward the way I should go. God has promised in Psalm 32:8, "I will instruct thee and teach thee in the way which thou shalt go: I will guide thee with mine eye."

Follow him. He knows the way.

Prayer

Lord, guide my feet along the right roads today. Without your instructions, my feet are sure to wander.

Reflection

What is one choice I could make today to show that I'm choosing to walk toward the New Jerusalem?

7

"I'M BETTER'N YOU!"

Isaiah 14:11-23; Luke 1:46-55

atthan and his cousin Kendrick, who's a year older, were playing with a jump rope the other day. They were pretending the length of pink rope was a corded telephone, and they each held one end to an ear and adopted an affected British accent as they hollered back and forth.

"How are you?" Matthan asked, to which Kendrick replied, "I'm better'n you!"

This did not please Matthan at all. "No!" he yelled. "I'm better'n you!"

They spent a minute or two in a heated go-around. "No. I'm better'n you!" "No! I am better'n you!" This was vastly amusing to Laverne and me as we listened in on the debate.

Although it was amusing, I later went about my work while pondering human nature, the old Adamic inclination toward pride and evil that is born into every person, not one soul missed. It makes each of us want to stand tall and announce "I'm better'n you." Perhaps we do so with words and actions that are veiled and civilized and thinly coated with a polite veneer. But the meaning is the same.

Isaiah 14:13-14 tells why Lucifer had fallen from heaven. "For thou hast said in thine heart . . . I will exalt my throne above the stars of God. . . . I will be like the most High."

Lucifer's issue was also pride. He wanted to be like the most high God. He too wanted to say, "I'm better'n you." Because of his proud heart, he was cast out of heaven. We also need to learn to control those proud hearts of ours.

Twice we're told, "God resisteth the proud, but giveth grace to the humble (James 4:6; 1 Peter 5:5), which reinforces what we're told in Proverbs 6:16-17: the Lord hates a proud look. He hates a proud heart too, yet the unruly heart of humankind, almost from birth, wants to say, "I'm better'n you."

I find that meditating on the vastness of God's creation—and acknowledging the unfathomable depths and widths and heights of God's creator mind which brought all this into being by a single uttered command—makes me feel very small indeed. In fact, it wipes away any desire to feel proud. It generates instead a feeling of awe that makes me see myself in my true light—I am nothing if I have not God.

Phillip Keller, in his book *David: The Shepherd King*, writes, "It is not who I am that matters half as much as *Whose* I am."[6]

When I begin to grasp this, everything comes into perspective. Who I am does not matter, nor do my achievements, pedigree, or background. Having God within my heart is what matters. That and serving God as the Lord and Master of my life.

Those who are truly God's children lose that desire to announce, either with words or deeds, "I'm better'n you." They know that being a forgiven child of the Most High is all that will matter at the end anyhow, and they want every other person to find that grace and love and forgiveness too. For in true humility of heart one finds the greatest depths of peace.

Prayer

Lord, I know that you resist the proud and shower your grace on the humble person. I need your help daily, even hourly, to become truly humble in heart.

Reflection

How could I serve someone else today by being humble and willing to be used of God?

1

BLUEBERRY THE CAT

Romans 12

Blueberry the cat thinks he is very important. His superiority oozes from every massive inch of him. After he had established his dominance on our premises, he stalked back and forth along the lane, daring any of the neighborhood cats to challenge his supremacy. Oh yes, Blueberry the cat thinks he is very important.

Stretched between the barn and shop is a six-foot-high length of chain link to keep the horses in the pasture. Blueberry learned to climb that fence, hoisting his large bulk up one side and painstakingly inching down the other. He always looked pained when he did it, as if this manner of negotiating a fence were beneath his dignity, but it needed to be done. It was part of the area he patrolled.

One day Laverne removed all the chain link except a single five-foot wide section beside the barn. Soon afterward I saw Blueberry, enormous as ever and still looking pained, climb over that section paw by paw. He inched down the other side and walked away, fur ruffled.

The reason we laughed was because if he had stepped a foot to the right, he could have paraded around the chain link without ruffling a hair. The rest of the fence was gone.

And we did laugh. Blueberry the cat had a very small brain, we said, and his pomposity became funnier than ever.

The apostle Paul's words in Galatians 6:3 could certainly be applied to Blueberry: "For if a man think himself to be something, when he is nothing, he deceiveth himself."

But on the other hand, Blueberry was just being a cat and following cat instincts. He is but an animal; even though we certainly enjoy him, in a few more years he will be gone. What does it matter how he conducts himself during these few fleeting years?

Paul's words were written for people with eternal souls, to you and me and everyone who has ever lived. Perhaps sometimes I'm sort of like Blueberry, doing things that look as absurd as climbing over a six-foot fence instead of taking a step to the right to walk around it. In what ways am I deceiving myself?

I do it whenever I take the credit for things I couldn't do if God were not giving me life and breath. "For in him we live, and move, and have our being" (Acts 17:28).

Whenever I think too much of myself, I'm forgetting that everything I am, everything I have, and everything around me, belongs to God. I wouldn't have another breath, another thought, if it weren't for the goodness of God. We know it can all vanish or change in an instant. If I can't even think a good thought without his help, how can I have any reason to be proud?

In verse 3 of today's Scripture reading, Paul addresses this problem once again: the problem that people (and animals) have of thinking too much of themselves. "For I say . . . to every man that is among you, not to think of himself more highly than he ought to think; but to think soberly, according as God hath dealt to every man the measure of faith."

If I think soberly of the things God has done for me by giving me life and then a chance to believe and obey and obtain life eternal, I don't have as much time to think about other, more earthly things.

And what God has done for me he has also done for everyone else. Behind every face is an eternal soul for whom Christ died. He doesn't love any person more than me, nor anyone less.

And since he loves us all the same, we have no reason to think of ourselves "more highly than we ought."

Prayer

Take my heart, O God, and mold it into one where you and you alone are Lord and Master. Then help me to love everyone else as you have loved them.

Reflection

How can I yield my heart to God more fully today?

2

SOWING FERNS, REAPING WISTERIA

Matthew 5:38-48; Galatians 6:6-10

Ostrich ferns grow thick and green in the shade garden near the forest, and they multiply rapidly. Each spring the bank of ferns spreads farther into the woods.

I was working in the garden one day in early spring when a shop customer and his wife stopped to talk with me. They liked gardening too, and the man pointed across the lawn to the row of green that was visible beneath the trees. "Are those ferns?"

"Yes, would you like to have some?" I asked, eager to thin the heavy ranks of waving fronds.

They seemed glad to accept my gift, and we exchanged some garden stories. They noticed the thick, still-dormant vine sprawling over a small building nearby and asked whether it was a wisteria. "No, that's a trumpet vine," I said. "I'd like to have a wisteria there someday." I pointed to a small start about the size of a pencil that I had planted behind the building. "If that will grow."

They gazed at it, too polite to mention that it looked anemic and tired of life before it had even begun.

I forgot about it as soon as they left. But the next week they brought me a wisteria plant in a container so huge I could barely lift it. They dropped it off in front of the shop and Laverne told me about it later.

I went out to examine it and stood staring at the curling vines that were leafed out, hearty and green and ready to grow. "You really do reap what you sow," I thought.

Not that I had been doubting this. But it had been a week when the bad seemed to overwhelm the good, and I was struggling with an issue of forgiveness. The wisteria leaves rippled in the breeze and appeared to be whispering: "Be not deceived; God is not mocked: for whatsoever a man soweth, that shall he also reap" (Galatians 6:7).

Galatians 6:9 adds, "And let us not be weary in well doing: for in due season we shall reap, if we faint not."

Don't give up, Paul says. We shall reap. Someday.

After all, very seldom does it come back as swiftly and suddenly as the ferns I exchanged for a wisteria. But what we sow we can count on reaping. Someday. Sooner or later.

Which would be nice to ponder if I always sowed kindness, generosity, graciousness, love. But I'm only human, and more times than I care to remember, I've found myself sowing seeds that sprout into ugly weeds. Unforgiveness. Anger. Greed. Envy. Selfishness. Gossip.

And then that is what I also find when I reap.

Someone has said, "We get out of life exactly what we put into it." That old saying, like many others, is based on a Bible truth. No one slips around the law of sowing and reaping, even if it might seem so for a time.

Often the stakes are higher than a few ferns exchanged for a wisteria. However, if I want to reap kindness and love, that's what I must sow. If I sow unkindness and gossip and hate, why am I surprised to get that in return?

Prayer

Lord, I want to sow seeds of love and understanding, yet so often I fail. Help me to get up and try again instead of becoming discouraged and giving up.

Reflection

How can I sow one kind act today?

3

THE DASH BETWEEN

Revelation 1; 1 Corinthians 15:51-58

Birth is by God's design. All life is his and is in his hands. He chooses when and where we're born and into what circumstances, family, religion, and country. Death is also God's. After all, he conquered it. As 1 Corinthians 15:54 says, "Death is swallowed up in victory."

But in between the first and last years are those years that will be signified on my gravestone by a simple little mark, a dash between the two dates that are the decrees of God.

"I am Alpha and Omega, the beginning and the ending," the Lord says in Revelation 1:8. And again in the same book, 22:13, "I am Alpha and Omega, the first and the last."

Oswald Chambers, in *Shade of His Hand*, comments, "It is in the middle that human choices are made; the beginning and the end remain with God. The decrees of God are birth and death, and in between those limits man makes his own distress or joy."[7]

I didn't chose to be born, nor do I know the hour of my death. My first hour was almost four decades ago. I have no way of knowing if the latter is to be in four days, or in another four decades.

"In between those limits," Chambers reminds us, "man makes his own distress or joy."

How can this be? How can I find joy when bad things are woven into that dash, and so much of life is out of my control?

God never promises happiness on this earth. He gives joy instead to the heart that is fully focused on him. His joy is a kind of serene and quiet peace that the world would counterfeit in any number of ways and call happiness.

The days we live are a mere dash between the two dates that will mark our sunrise and our sunset. The great rush of years as time sweeps on often seems to make it an actual dash indeed. We have little to say, sometimes, in how things turn out. But one choice we do get to make. We choose whether we will set our hearts on the things of God or on the things offered by the prince of the world. In this way we manufacture our own distress or joy.

Thomas Carlyle described it like this: "One Life; a little gleam of Time between two Eternities."[8]

What will we do with that little gleam of time which is given us? How will we repay God for that gift, those years of the dash? By serving him with love and obedience? Or by rejecting the message of the cross and the invitation of the crucified?

He gives us the right to decide.

And to those who have chosen to believe in him, he says in Revelation 1:17: "Fear not; I am the first and the last."

Fear not. He orchestrated our beginning. He will see to the end. Fear not.

Prayer

Lord, I have chosen to serve you during these years between the dash. Please do not let me turn away from the vows I have made to you.

Reflection

Today is the beginning of the rest of my life. How can I strengthen my desire to follow Jesus?

4

OBEDIENCE

John 10; Hebrews 11:8-19

O
ne summer evening when Alisha was about five years old, she was sitting on a large rock near the edge of the lawn. She was waiting until Laverne and Cody were ready to play a game with her.

From where he was standing a short distance away, Laverne was able to see beneath the edge of the rock. What he saw alarmed him.

"Alisha," he said, "come to me."

And without protest or question, Alisha obeyed. When she was safely on the grass beside him, Laverne ran for a shovel. He had seen underneath the rock the smooth copper coils of a snake, which turned out to be not one but three copperheads.

It made my blood run cold when they told me. It makes my blood run cold to this day. What if Alisha had not obeyed promptly? What if she had kicked or protested? What if she had decided not to listen to her daddy's voice that particular time?

Obedience is a difficult journey. As parents, we're required to teach our children obedience in a loving way ("Children, obey your parents," Ephesians 6:1), but I suspect any parent knows that as we go about teaching our children obedience, the task is sometimes made harder by our own stubborn natures. Are we submissive to God's authority first, and submissive to those he has placed in authority over us? If not, how can we expect our children to willingly comply with us?

John 10:27 says, "My sheep hear my voice, and I know them, and they follow me." To follow God, we must know his voice, and to know his voice, we must learn to obey his commands. Not always because we understand exactly why he is asking a certain thing of us, but because we know we must obey the voice of our Shepherd.

Hebrews 11:8 reads, "By faith Abraham, when he was called to go out . . . obeyed; and he went out, not knowing wither he went."

Abraham obeyed God's voice. He didn't know why God asked him to leave his homeland. He just obeyed. God knew the reason, and Abraham submitted.

Alisha didn't know why her father was asking her to leave her comfortable perch on the rock. She only knew he called, and she obeyed. Her prompt obedience almost certainly spared her the painful consequences of what could have happened.

Recently I took particular notice of Hebrews 5:8-9: "Though [Jesus] were a Son, yet learned he obedience by the things which he suffered; And being made perfect, he became the author of eternal salvation unto all them that obey him."

Jesus was perfect in obedience, for he obeyed God in everything. It says he learned it "by the things which he suffered." Should we expect anything less? The things we suffer can sometimes be traced directly to our own self-will and disobedience. Even if our suffering is the result of someone else's disobedience, we can learn submission and surrender through it.

Jesus doesn't promise that we'll understand everything we're asked to do or submit to. He does say he holds the eternal salvation of "all them that obey him."

We can run away and refuse to listen. Or we can obey and run toward the sound of his voice.

Prayer

Lord, please show me how to be more obedient to you today.

Reflection

What is one thing God is asking of me? How can I respond positively?

5

HAPPINESS IS

John 13

Everyone is seeking happiness in some way. The U.S. Declaration of Independence, written in 1776, promises "Life, Liberty, and the Pursuit of Happiness" to every citizen and permits each of us to decide how to find it.

Where do you look for happiness? Where do I pursue it? Is it found in having lots of money? If it is, why are some of the wealthiest people also some of the unhappiest?

Is it found in fame and popularity? If so, why have so many famous people, perhaps in an attempt to flee the profound emptiness of their existence, taken their own lives?

Some believe power and authority translate into happiness. Others think good looks and many possessions will make them happy. Still others search for some sense of happiness in addictions that leave them more miserable than fulfilled.

I searched my Bible and found a different understanding of happiness. In John 13:17, Jesus says, "If ye know these things, happy are ye if ye do them."

It's the only place I can find where Jesus made any promise of happiness to his followers. The verse tells us that if we know the things he asks us to do (they're in the Bible) and we do them, we'll be happy. And this happiness comes quietly as peace, tranquility, and hope.

I found only a few more references to *happy* in my King James Version. Here are three:

Behold, we count them happy which endure. (James 5:11)

But and if ye suffer for righteousness' sake, happy are ye.
(1 Peter 3:14)

If ye be reproached for the name of Christ, happy are ye; for
the spirit of glory and of God resteth upon you. (1 Peter 4:14)

Obviously, as Christians seeking to be citizens of heaven someday,
our understanding of happiness is not quite that which we find in
any dictionary—or the Declaration of Independence.

We're happy . . . if we can endure to the end, for that is when the
crown of life will be presented.

We're happy . . . if we suffer for righteousness' sake. Instead of
turning away from God, how much am I willing to suffer?

We're happy . . . when reproached for the name of Christ. Will
I stand strong for my convictions even when serving Jesus Christ
would cause me to suffer as the earliest Christians did?

Some translations use the word *blessed* instead of *happy* in
these verses.

So to be happy, to be called blessed, we endure. Whether it's suffering or reproach or ridicule or something else entirely. We endure
to the end.

Jesus endured the cross for me. I endure for him whatever he asks
of me.

Prayer

Lord, when I want to be happy,
remind me to seek it your way,
and not necessarily mine.

Reflection

How could I seek to find happiness God's way today?

6

SOUL GARDENING

John 15:1-11

Each spring, anything seems possible again as I wander along
the flower-bordered paths where plants are awakening. I
dream of perfect gardens with large flowers and abundant fruit, vegetables with no blemishes, and rain when we need it. Even though
reality invades the vision eventually, I dream anyway.

Then I think of the things God would like to grow in my heart
garden: fruit of the Spirit such as love, joy, peace, patience, kindness,
and goodness. Plus faith, humility, and self-control. What blights
and droughts and diseases are preventing me from performing to
my full potential, and how can I cut them out of my life? Does the
Master Gardener ever grow weary of the chastening and pruning I
require? And how grateful I should be that he never gives up! For
no ground is too hard, dry, or stony for God to make beautiful with
flowers and fruit.

It doesn't happen overnight, or even in one season. I spend a lot
of time walking through the gardens, watching the performance of
the plants, studying their progress, deciding what each one needs.
What can remain and what must be removed? Some of the plants
must be divided so they can continue to grow. Others are dead.
My goal for the gardens is always to make them better, and there's
always work to do.

Does God work in a similar way in my life? Does he watch over
the progress I'm making as I grow as a Christian? Does he send peri-
ods of drought to help me sink my roots deeper into the soil of faith
and trust? What will he trim from my life because it is not bearing

him fruit? Are the rainy seasons reminders for me to draw closer to the solid Rock that he wants to be in my life?

God is always vigilant when he watches over my life, and he is always working to bring good things out of what were once barren places in my soul. I know he wants to help me grow to be more like him, and that the pruning he does will eventually shape me more fully into a woman who brings him glory.

I'm not always fond of his methods as he prunes my soul and discards the parts that hinder my growth and bear no fruit. But even when it seems hard, I still believe it's necessary and that it will allow me to bloom abundantly for him on some tomorrow.

Prayer

I don't always understand your ways, Lord, but I do believe you are working in my heart to make it better. Let me help and not hinder the progress.

Reflection

What is growing in my heart that needs pruning today?

7

MORE PRUNING

John 15:12-17

As a gardener, I know that right now my garden still needs two things to make it better. More time and more pruning. Both can be tiresome, and the pruning becomes downright painful sometimes.

But prune I do, and I haul away debris by the wheelbarrow load. Shrubs and roses look much improved with all the dead and winter-frozen branches chopped off and their shape neatly maintained. I trim away old foliage and lightly rake the winter mulch from around the plants. The warm spring sun caresses the dormant stems that remain and coaxes new life from the roots buried deep in the soil.

With a little more time, the shrubs and roses will uncurl tiny green leaves and sprout buds by the hundreds. The new and lavish displays of spring flowers will soon be breathtaking.

But they would not be half so nice if I were to let them grow scraggly and untamed and neglected. The hard pruning I give them is precisely what they need to make them so lovely later.

When God is at work pruning away the outgrown or unnecessary areas of my life, I sometimes cringe away from his hands, away from the blades of the shears he uses. Away from the pain that occurs when I'm required to give up something I still want to keep. Why do I do this when I believe the work he's doing is for the good of my soul? I know I too need regular pruning to bring new spiritual growth into my heart.

I cringe because all pruning demands a degree of pain. Sometimes it's a lot, sometimes it's less, but it always hurts. I'd rather have the flowers, the fruit, the good results without the pruning, and I'd rather have them immediately.

But kindly, gently, God reminds me of the areas in my life that need more light. More pruning. Do I have a harmful attitude that needs to go? Are there sinful places that need to be cut away? And what about my habits? Do any make me uncomfortable when I imagine God examining them?

It will take time, but eventually this kind of pruning also brings the desired results. If it's uncomfortable now, I must remember that I will bloom again. And the flowers and fruit will be better than ever before.

Prayer

Dear God, it hurts when you prune away the overgrown and unnecessary places in my life. I need your help to remember that, in time, this pruning will bloom with new growth and fresh blossoms.

Reflection

How can I begin to prune a bad habit today?

1

PRUNING HEARTS

John 15:18-27

*N*ot only does pruning branches play an essential part of gardening, but so does thinning roots by dividing them. Each spring, I divide more plants again or dig out others. I tend to crowd and overplant, so this is a necessary part of gardening for me.

Roots need room to grow underground, room to flourish and breathe and spread. They need enough surrounding space to let in air and moisture. And when the roots are dug from the soil and chopped apart, I must decide what to replant, what to move elsewhere, and what to discard.

There are times I must clean out my house too. I find that my plants can't flourish without adequate space, and in the same way I begin to feel crowded and stifled if my house is cluttered with too much stuff. My house needs occasional pruning—aka decluttering—in every room. Then I can move and breathe and absorb air and sunlight again.

Sometimes I must sort through my life in this manner too, decluttering my heart. It means discarding worn-out ideas, goals, and dreams, as well as any notions or opinions or presumptions that time has proved false, weak, or even harmful.

Just as I prune the roots of the plants that have become too crowded, I have to prune from my heart anything that is worthless or lacking in qualities that build up. I have to make space for God's air and sunlight to filter in—that is, time for prayer and praise and worship and personal and family devotions. I have to clean the clutter from my soul to make room for more of God and his Word. If I don't make sure to prune my heart, it won't take long for the rush of living to drown out the quiet voice of God. I have to set aside a space that's devoted to God's Word and prayer, and then prune relentlessly when other activities and cares encroach on that time and that part of my heart.

Undoubtedly, God still sees many areas where I need even more pruning in my heart and life. After all, he is the Gardener who works so patiently in the soil of my heart and tends his seeds with constant care. He is waiting for his garden to bear fruit too, pruning until the sunlight can penetrate the shaded areas, sending dark days of rain and occasional flooding, and always, always coaxing new growth from painful places where the old has been pruned away.

It's a continual process, this one, and will take all the years of my life.

Prayer

Even when it hurts, Lord, I want you to prune in my heart so that I may grow ever more pleasing to you. I am grateful you are patient when the new growth is slow to appear.

Reflection

What is one thing I could work at pruning from my heart?

2

SERVICE

Matthew 25:31-46

When Mother Teresa died on September 5, 1997, she left behind all the possessions she had accumulated in her eighty-seven years on earth. Those possessions were two saris (a woman's garment that is worn in India) and the bucket she used to wash in.

Mother Teresa was outstandingly poor in possessions, but she was incredibly rich in service and love. The mission in Calcutta, which she founded and where she worked, took in persons who were destitute and homeless. Mother Teresa would carry dying people in from the streets, wash diseased bodies, clean up filth, hand-feed the starving and weak and those with disabilities. No job was too dirty or lowly for her to tackle with her own hands.

Mother Teresa was the epitome of those to whom the King speaks in Matthew 25:40: "And the King shall answer and say unto them . . . as ye have done it unto one of the least of these my brethren, ye have done it unto me."

Mother Teresa's selflessness is an inspiration to every Christian woman who longs to be of service to her King.[9] But not everyone is able to travel to distant cities or to work in slums among the homeless. Can we still serve the King?

Indeed, our life is to be one extended act of service to God. And it can begin exactly where we are, today.

Elizabeth George, in *Loving God with All Your Mind*, writes, "You see, I exist to serve [God] and his people according to the gifts he has given me and in the situations where he places me."[10]

Our brief life here is to serve God where he has placed us. One way to do that is to serve his people, and most often that work begins at home.

I quote Darlene Marie Wilkinson, who wrote *The Prayer of Jabez for Women*: "As wives, mothers, daughters, widows, or single women, the most important territory we are given is our loved ones and our closest friends. God doesn't ask us to neglect our home turf to go looking for greener pastures. . . . Instead, he helps us discover the amazing potential we have to impact the world right from our own living room."[11]

Mother Teresa's "living room" was the missions she founded, and their work still continues. She served God by caring for those around her wherever she was.

God asks some of us to serve him closer to home, in the kitchen or living room or classroom. In school and at church. Caring for our children and shepherding their souls. Preparing food and washing dishes and clothes. Telling others about him and his offer of a new and better life. Making sacrifices to help those who need it. Living with less and reaching out to the neighborhood around us.

Mother Teresa tackled one need and one person at a time. God expects us to do the same in the part of the world where he has put us. Perhaps our territory will never be as vast or as far-reaching as hers, but that is no excuse not to begin.

Prayer

Teach me to serve you, Lord, wherever I am and however I can. I want to learn that true service begins at home first and then widens to include everyone around me.

Reflection

How could I help a friend today? How could I help a stranger I meet?

3

IMPROVEMENTS

Genesis 2:8-17

I strolled through my flower and herb gardens one day in early spring. Warm and lengthening days were waking the earth, and the beds were full of new growth. Daffodils and grape hyacinths grew side by side with the chartreuse leaves of lady's mantle and gray-green catmint.

Roses were unfurling tiny reddish leaves, and herbs and perennials alike were burgeoning with new life. It was a splendid day, and I was watching the world come alive again.

But even as I strolled through the gardens, observing the way the plants were responding to the sunshine and delighting in the progress I noticed, I saw things that needed improvement. There was work to be done.

Winter had been hard and cold, and it had left its imprint. Here and there a shrub was dead, or at least frozen to the ground. The wooden frame of the grape arbor was rotting and would have to be removed. There were rocks to be replaced along the edging, and perennials to divide and replant.

The work would never be completely finished. As long as the gardens were alive, they would need careful tending, surveillance, and a watchful eye ready to spot pests, diseases, and troublesome areas.

I thought about the gardens God has planted in our hearts, the seeds he has sowed there, the growth he nurtures so lovingly. He sees our progress and observes even the smallest struggle toward light and new growth.

I think he too delights in his gardens—the ones he wants to tend in our hearts. He watches over those seeds and plants with a careful eye and deals out adequate portions of rain and sunshine to sustain life and growth.

Yet his work is never done. As long as I have life and breath, I also have areas in my heart garden that need improvement. Some of the enemy's seeds settle down in a dark corner and begin to grow. Before I quite know what has happened, good-sized weeds are thriving there.

Those must be painfully dug out and discarded. Old habits are always stealthily trying to sneak back in and find a foothold somewhere.

My garden is never so good that it doesn't have problem areas, places that need more work.

And the areas in my heart where God wants to grow his fruit of love and peace, hope and joy, are never complete. His refining work of improvement will take from now until eternity.

Prayer

Lord, you can see all the places in my heart that need more work. Give me the courage to begin.

Reflection

How could I begin to improve the garden in my heart today?

4

GRATITUDE
AND BEETLES

Colossians 3:12-17; 1 Thessalonians 5:18

There are hundreds of ladybugs lying on the window frames and sills of the three west-facing windows of my house. These aren't the beneficial ladybugs I like to see hard at work in the gardens each summer. No, these are imported imposters that resemble the true ladybug, but which have become a homemaker's bad dream. They crawl into every crack of the house when it gets cold in the fall. Then they creep out again each spring.

Like now. By the thousands and for weeks on end. Does "giving thanks always for all things unto God and the Father in the name of our Lord Jesus Christ" (Ephesians 5:20) mean being grateful for these beetles too?

I'm assuming it does. It's just taking me a while. I'm moving toward gratitude for these bugs one slow step at a time.

Corrie ten Boom was a woman who was sent by the Nazis to an extermination camp at Ravensbrück, Germany, during one of the last years of World War II. She and her family suffered terribly at the hands of the SS officers, not because they were Jews, but because they had provided aid to those who were.

Corrie and her sister Betsie were housed in filthy barracks with little light and even less plumbing. The women prisoners were each assigned a sleeping platform. These were narrow spaces that were stacked one above the other up to the ceiling. The thin bedding was dirty and rancid, but even worse, it was swarming with fleas.

Corrie and Betsie struggled here. For survival, but also for a reason to give thanks. Betsie quoted 1 Thessalonians 5:18—"In every thing give thanks: for this is the will of God in Christ Jesus concerning you"—and encouraged Corrie to find a reason to be grateful. For a time, Corrie insisted that gratitude was impossible in their situation, and no wonder. Can I blame her? Not at all. It takes far less to make me start complaining.

But Betsie persisted, and they began their journey toward gratitude. They thanked God that they were together, that they still had their Bible, that the guards didn't interfere when they gathered with their fellow prisoners to read chapters from it aloud.

But still Corrie felt that thanking God for the fleas was not an option. Thank him for the existence of those swarms of miserable bugs?

Not until some time later did they learn that those large numbers of fleas were the reason the guards seldom disturbed them or broke up their Bible readings. The fleas acted as a barrier between the prisoners and those who guarded them. There was a reason after all to thank God for the fleas.

Trials of all kinds are a part of life, and no one escapes them. But God has asked us to give thanks in all things. He knows we need these trials to help us grow stronger.

He has a reason for the small, vexing fleas too. And imported beetles. He doesn't say we have to understand them first. He just says, "Give thanks."

Prayer

Today when I thank you, O God, help me to be grateful even for the small annoyances. May I learn that how I respond to these trials is an opportunity to become stronger in you.

Reflection

What is "biting like a flea" in my life today?

5

OLD FAITHFULS

3 John

There are some plants in my gardens that I appreciate more with every passing season.

It's not the roses, those high-maintenance, prickly things that would as soon jab and scratch as not. Though I love them dearly, I don't deny that they take much labor and sometimes give little in return.

It's not the peonies, which burst open for a brief, glorious flaunting of showy colors. Though magnificent while they last, they fade too soon and keel over in the first wind or rain.

Nor is it the powerful vines and ground covers that serve a needed purpose by crawling over untidy spots, yet which desire above all else to control and conquer. It takes a firm hand to check them, and they must constantly be pruned, cut back, and dug out.

And it's not the annuals, with their nonstop blooms in a rainbow of colors. Though they fill their spots admirably, the first frost halts them in their tracks and they curl up and die.

The plants I really appreciate, the ones that inspire my devotion, are my old faithfuls. Those quiet, steady perennials that calmly fill their places year after year. The daylilies and coneflowers and the silvermound. The phlox and hostas and columbine, and many more.

These are the sturdy, dependable pillars of the garden that grow more beautiful with every passing season. They are the backbone of the flower beds, the stabilizers that set the pace.

When I stop to think about it, the people I most admire are like that too. The kind who quietly stay in their place, making their life and the lives of those around them more beautiful every year.

They are the faithful ones who calmly serve in the roles where they are called, those who are dependable, loyal, and trustworthy, and of whom it can be said "Beloved, thou doest faithfully whatsoever thou doest" (3 John verse 5) rather than "For he that wavereth is like a wave of the sea driven with the wind and tossed" (James 1:6).

These are the kind of people God can use in his kingdom, the ones who are faithfully doing whatever he requires of them. These are the ones I admire more each year.

Then comes the thought: It's not enough to admire them. I must become like that too. Reliable, steadfast, and devoted to God's will and his Word.

Faithful. That's what he expects me to be.

Prayer

O God, you know my heart and its longings. Please help me to remain faithful to all you ask of me.

Reflection

What plant am I most like now? Is this good or not so good?

6

LETTUCE OR ROSES OR WEEDS

Matthew 13:1-23

The ground where I grow my roses must be carefully prepared. Their roots go deep, and the topsoil on this hilltop doesn't. So I have to spend a lot of time grubbing around in the dirt first, digging large holes and filling them with better soil. And I place lasagna-type layers around the holes to extend the space.

I could plant the roses without preparing the soil first, but they wouldn't grow as well. Some would give up and sulk, others would give up and die. They like good, deep, rich earth into which to sink their roots.

Where I plant lettuce, I worry not so much about depth as about having a fertile half foot or so of topsoil. The tiny lettuce seeds flourish there, and in a few weeks they'll have produced a crop of salad greens for our meals. Their roots are shallower than those of the roses, but they still require good soil. They just need all their nutrients in the top few inches.

And where the soil lies empty and uncared for, where I plant nothing at all, weeds quickly fill every corner. They need no help, no encouragement, and certainly no soil preparation. Weeds grow with no effort.

"Gloom we have always with us," writes Barbara Holland, "a rank and sturdy weed, but joy requires tending."[12]

Gloom and weeds, like sin, need no extra help on our part. They just grow.

But if I want a harvest of some kind, if I want roses or lettuce leaves, a joyful heart or fruitful spirit, it's going to take some work for that to happen.

If the soil in my heart is hard or sin-clodded or full of gloom, I'll have to dig deep to remove it. And I'll have to fill my heart with fertile and fruit-producing activities. What I grow in that garden is largely up to me.

Because whether I grow roses or lettuce, tomatoes or daisies, the garden that's flourishing within my heart is going to depend a great deal on how I nourish it.

And if I make no effort to grow spiritually, if I ignore God and the good news of Jesus Christ, the weeds in my heart will grow fast. I've watched weeds take over in any garden I've planted outdoors, and in no time at all. If I'm not on the job to remove them, they will crowd out any of the good seeds I've planted.

Sin can take over a life just as fast. It requires no tending. "For the imagination [thought or intent] of [a person's] heart is evil from his youth" (Genesis 8:21).

What I grow in my heart is up to me.

Prayer

Lord, I want my heart to be full of good things. I need you to be the Master Gardener there.

Reflection

What seeds am I planting in my heart today?

7

HYDRANGEA FLOWERS

1 Corinthians 12

Along the west side of the porch, I planted a row of hydrangeas. They sank their roots deep into the cool, moist soil, and
now they bloom with enthusiasm each summer.

Limelight grows there, a Vanilla Strawberry, an Endless Summer,
and a few feet away, a Pinky Winky. Their blooms are magnificent.
Most are more than a foot wide, and some exceed two feet across at
their widest part. As flowers go, these are showstoppers.

But if you were to take one branch and examine it closely, as I
did one day, you would see that every one of these huge blossoms is
composed of hundreds of tiny, four-petaled flowerets. These florets
each contribute in a small way to the composite flower head.

By themselves, these miniature florets would nearly go unnoticed.
But together they create a masterpiece of almost unsurpassed beauty.

The little bit of good one person can do also seems to go unnoticed in the great swelling tide of human need. Saying one prayer,
helping one child, feeding one hungry person, sewing one blanket
to send overseas—what does my one small contribution help when
millions are in need?

Or, when we serve God in one small, out-of-the-way corner of
the planet, what contribution to the universe, church, community, or
family is that? Does it mean anything?

Of course it does! No life stands unnoticed before God, and no
small effort to serve him is overlooked. Not one of us, alone, could
do much to help others. But when we work together there is no end
to the good we might do.

The smallest florets on the hydrangea flower head are filling their place and contributing to the whole just as surely as the largest. If one were to lose heart and drop from the branch because it felt unnoticed or unappreciated, it would leave an empty space. If one became discontented with its place and went searching for a more prominent spot, the flower head would lose its harmony and pattern.

Fortunately, flowers don't act like that. But people do.

Yet verse 18 in today's Scripture reminds us, "But now hath God set the members every one of them in the body, as it hath pleased him."

We are where we are because it has pleased God to put us there.

Today's Scripture continues, "But now are they many members, yet but one body. And the eye cannot say unto the hand, I have no need of thee: nor again the head to the feet, I have no need of you" (verses 20-21).

Every floret on the hydrangea flower is needed to make a perfect blossom. When each one fills its place, they make a lovely picture.

Every person in the family, community, and church is placed where God is pleased to have him or her. Each one is needed to form the whole. And when we're all working together to serve God, he can take even our smallest efforts and multiply them to bless more people than we could ever imagine.

Prayer

Today I want to fill my small corner with love for you, O God. Teach me how you would have me do that.

Reflection

How can I serve God in the corner of the world where God has placed me?

1

MATTHAN'S WATER

John 7:33-39; Isaiah 58:11-14; Jeremiah 31:12

*M*atthan filled a small toy bucket with water one day. He used it to submerge his plastic animals, washing them in the process. The water, which had been clean at first, had taken on a distinctly cloudy shade. The more he played in it, the dirtier it became.

Then Matthan decided he was thirsty. And the toy bucket was full of water, just ready to drink.

"Oh, don't drink that," I said. "I'll get you some fresh, clean water." And so saying, I filled a glass and took it to him.

But either I was too slow or he was too impatient. Or maybe he just wanted to find out how the cloudy water in his pail would taste. Because he had already lifted it to his mouth and gulped some of it down.

I poured the glass of fresh water into the sink and asked myself why we also prefer the muddy, brown waters when we try to quench the thirst inside our hearts. And why we think the sinful world around us has something to still the restless longings for purpose and fulfillment when Jesus offers us clean, fresh water that would quiet the ceaseless searching for something to satisfy.

"If any man thirst, let him come unto me, and drink," Jesus invited the multitudes over two thousand years ago (John 7:37). He's still inviting the multitudes. To anyone who will listen, he's still saying, "Come to me. I can satisfy the thirst in your heart. I can fill the empty places. I can heal the soul that is sick with sin."

He does ask one thing of us. He asks that we stop trying to satisfy our thirst with the dirty, cloudy, soiled waters of this world. He asks us to repent of and forsake our sins. He wants to give us the pure, clean, refreshing water that brings rest and peace and hope, but he won't do that as long as we insist on drinking out of the filthy bucket Satan is holding.

God never uses force to bring anyone into his kingdom. He makes it clear that we must desire him and his Spirit more than we desire the tainted and perverted things that Satan would deceive us into thinking bring lasting pleasure and fulfillment.

First we must desire the fresh, the pure, the clean. We must want it more than we want to dabble in the murky and polluted waters around us.

Prayer

The more I learn to drink of the clean waters you offer, Lord, the less I desire to taste the muddied ones. Show me how to use discernment when I seek something to satisfy my thirst.

Reflection

How can I choose to drink clean water today?

2

HOUSES THAT LAST

Psalm 127; 2 Corinthians 5:1-8

When I entered the house, I noticed the series of deep scratches in the wood trim beside the door on the porch. It looked like the work of a sharp tool in the hands of a little boy.

Although we built our house a mere dozen years ago, it is already showing signs of wear and decay. Rain gutters need periodic repair, scratches have appeared here and there on walls and floors. A leak behind the shower caused a patch of wood to rot. And all the children, as they learned to write, were overcome by a powerful urge to sign their name somewhere on a wall or windowsill.

As soon as a house is roofed and furnished it becomes inclined to decay. Even if built to withstand rainstorms and winter winds, most houses will last only a few centuries. And that is with continual repairs and upkeep.

I think I'm showing some signs of wear and tear too. Extra pounds have crept on, wrinkles have begun to form; I've acquired reading glasses and, of all things, I'm finding some gray strands in my hair. Things like this remind me I'm not as young as I remember being.

The change and wear would be worse if it wasn't that God has promised something far better than this to his children. "For we know that if our earthly house [that is, physical body] . . . were dissolved, we have a building of God, an house not made with hands, eternal in the heavens" (2 Corinthians 5:1).

That is what God's children focus on as houses and bodies wear out. This life is not all there is. There's another one coming, of which God has promised, "Behold, I make all things new" (Revelation

21:5). Somewhere we have a house that will never grow old and a body that will be young forever.

Wrinkles on faces and scratches in wood are only for a time. Christians are more concerned about the wrinkles and scratches in their souls, about the things that separate them from God. Our souls need repair too. We need repentance and confession of sins, healing of bitterness, forgiveness of those who have wronged us, and acceptance of grace. We need to strive always to live a life that is righteous before God.

God has eternal homes ready and waiting. He has issued an invitation to each of us and has promised new and everlasting bodies too. What he wants to do today is help us prepare to reach those homes and inherit those bodies.

Prayer

Lord, make me willing to surrender my entire life to you. In exchange, you have promised eternity with you, and houses and bodies that never wear out.

Reflection

What do I look forward to in heaven?

3

DOING GOD'S WILL

Matthew 7:21-23; 12:49-50; Luke 22:41-43

Sometimes I ask my children to do a chore they'd rather not. It happens quite often, actually, and they occasionally make their displeasure plain.

Oh, they do the job, but they do it with sighs and frowns and complaints. Even Matthan is capable of grumbling: "I don't want to set the table again!"

And Cody: "You mean I have to stack firewood? I wanted to explore in the valley." Or Alisha: "I have to bake cookies again?" Their complaining robs us all of any joy in the work.

"Some of us are slow to do God's will," writes Oswald Chambers in *The Moral Foundations of Life*. "We do it as if our shoes were iron and lead; we do it with a great sigh and with the corners of our mouths down, as if His will were the most arduous thing on earth. But when our wills are rectified and brought into harmony with God, it is a delight, a superabounding joy, to do God's will."[13]

That's not the only place where Chambers writes on this subject. In *Our Brilliant Heritage*, he says, "Doing God's will is never hard. The only thing that is hard is *not* doing His will. . . . God's will is hard only when it comes up against our stubbornness. When once God has His way, we are emancipated into the very life of God."[14]

What happens when the children complain when I ask them to do something that conflicts with what they wanted to do? If they grumble and frown and trudge with dragging feet to do the assigned duty, they certainly make themselves unhappy. I feel annoyed. Perhaps they need more chastening.

But how do I respond when God asks me to do something I don't want to do?

Well, then I can see why my children respond as they do. Because sometimes I too frown and sigh, drag my feet, and whine, "Lord, you have asked a very hard thing of me. I didn't want to do this! I wanted to continue what I was doing."

My children don't always respond to work with complaints. Sometimes they come running, and work cheerfully. They ask what else they can do to help me. This makes me happy, and their willingness gives them joyful hearts. They reap happiness along with my blessings and praise because they were obedient.

When I respond to God's authority with a willing heart, I discover that his commands are not arduous or unreasonable. He gives joy and peace to anyone who responds with a cheerful "What more can I do?" instead of a whining "What more must I do?"

It's a daily challenge. But doing the will of God is not too hard, unless I insist on making it so.

Prayer

In my heart, I want to do your will, and to do it willingly. Continue to show me how to respond to you.

Reflection

In what way could I do God's will today?

4

WORKING FOR
THE LORD

Colossians 3:22-25

This morning I filled all the laundry lines with freshly washed dresses, shirts, towels, and socks, then drained the dirty gray water from the washing machine.

I boiled three dozen eggs and peeled them. I put some of them into pickled red beet juice to make red beet eggs. I also baked two small pans of brownies.

I swept a few floors and was, as always, amazed at the amount of dirt and dust and dried mud I collected.

I helped Matthan with his coat, and we walked to the barn to peer at a phoebe's nest that was perched on a beam high over our heads.

Much as I love being a mother and homemaker, there are days when the repetitious work seems trifling and unimportant. After all, most of those clean clothes will be dirty again before the end of the week. The food will disappear within a day or two. The floors will need to be swept again before the sun sets tonight.

Yet whenever I read Colossians 3, I find that the purpose for my work is clear. I am laboring for my family, that's true, but in a way I am also working for the Lord.

"And whatsoever ye do, do it heartily, as to the Lord, and not unto men" (verse 23).

To me, this means doing my work here at home willingly and with joy, delighting in the long lines of clean clothes dancing in the breeze, inhaling the scent of chocolate, watching the ruby juice settle around the milky-white eggs, smiling with Matthan as he points out the phoebe's nest. Serving the Lord doesn't always mean great deeds in distant places so much as it means doing the daily, at-home duties faithfully and well.

Verse 24 adds, "For ye serve the Lord Christ." It is the Lord Christ who has given us our places where we serve, and he asks that we work "heartily," doing what he has requested of us.

If I work for God, doing faithfully even the small, repetitious chores, "Ye shall receive the reward" (verse 24). But if I decide to ignore his commands and the place where he's asked that I serve him, the outcome is also clear.

"But he that doeth wrong shall receive for the wrong which he hath done: and there is no respect of persons" (verse 25).

There's no partiality. No excuses. Either I work for him or I don't. Either way, I'll be rewarded for my work.

Prayer

It is my heart's desire to serve you every day, Lord. Thank you for the fulfillment that comes from serving my family, for in this way I am also working for you.

Reflection

How can I work for the Lord today?

5

FAITH THROUGH THE FIERY FURNACE

Daniel 3:16-30

For some reason, Matthan likes being held by his ankles and swung upside down. Although he's now almost too heavy for me to do this to him, he will sometimes coax Laverne to grab him by the ankles and hoist him upward. Then Matthan hangs there upside down, squealing with delight as Laverne swings him back and forth.

"He's got a lot of confidence in me," Laverne remarked once when Matthan dangled fearlessly from his hands and demanded a longer session of viewing the world with his head inches from the floor.

And certainly Matthan had no fear of being dropped. He had perfect faith in his daddy.

Three men who also had perfect faith were Daniel's friends. When commanded to obey the king of the land rather than God, they chose to remain faithful to God. They had confidence in his power. This is how they replied:

> If it be so, our God whom we serve is able to deliver us from the burning fiery furnace, and he will deliver us out of thine hand, O king.

> But if not, be it known unto thee . . . that we will not serve thy gods. (Daniel 3:17-18)

> Listen to what they are saying: "God can save us from this fiery furnace. But even if he doesn't, we'll serve him anyway."

There is the pivotal point of faith. "God can heal my disease, restore my loss, protect my life, remove any danger and threats. But if he doesn't, I will trust him anyway."

Sometimes—quite often, actually—faith is tested in the fiery furnace of trials, as Shadrach, Meshach, and Abednego were tested in the book of Daniel. And if we could see clearly at those times, we might also be able to see Someone by our side, "walking in the midst of the fire . . . the form . . . like the Son of God" (verse 25). But because our eyes are so often blinded by smoke or tears, we stumble on, believing God is nowhere close.

At times, as he did with Daniel's three friends, God delivers us from those trials unharmed. But other times we emerge scarred, damaged, shell-shocked, stricken with pain and grief. The furnace has burned away life as we knew it, and the pain with which we view life makes it too hard to see clearly.

Sometimes the only thing left to do is to say, "Our God whom we serve is able to deliver us from this. But even if he doesn't, we will trust him anyway."

Prayer

I know you have my life in your hands, O God, and I don't have to know what is happening when you turn it upside down. Help me to trust you anyway.

Reflection

What is one area where I find it difficult to trust God completely?

6

THE FAITH CHAPTER

Hebrews 11

The first verse in Hebrews 11 defines faith as "the substance of things hoped for, the evidence of things not seen."

Faith is believing what we hope for. It is something that cannot be seen or even completely understood. If we could understand everything about it, it wouldn't be faith. It would be knowledge.

"But without faith it is impossible to please him: for he that cometh to God must believe that he *is*" (verse 6, italics mine).

A steadfast faith, a great depth of belief in God, is why the people mentioned in Hebrews 11 could endure their individual fiery trials. And by faith they lived their lives, and they "died in faith, not having received the promises, but having seen them afar off, and were persuaded of them" (verse 13).

Faith has to be a way of life, and a way of living that life. Because we're not going to understand everything that happens—or why—there are many things we must take on simple faith. Not because we have any answers to that age-old question, "Why?" but because we have faith that God does.

Each of the people mentioned in Hebrews 11 proved their faith. They had to live it. They had to believe God meant what he said, even when they didn't know why he said it. They needed to believe God knew what he was doing, and because they had faith in him, they didn't have to understand it.

Nor are they the only ones. I believe that God still tests each one of us today to see whether we'll stay faithful to him. To see if we will trust even when we can't see the reason or understand his methods.

This is what James Dobson says about faith: "Apparently, most believers are permitted to go through emotional and spiritual valleys that are designed to test their faith in the crucible of fire. Why? Because faith ranks at the top of God's system of priorities. Without it, He said, it is impossible to please Him."[15]

So it seems to me that faith is a choice. We can believe God is and is what he says, and can keep on believing that when nothing else makes sense.

Then, through faith, we can also look for "a city . . . whose builder and maker is God" (verse 10).

It will take faith to get there, plus a lot of determination to hold on to that faith. But in that city we will need faith no longer.

Because at last we'll be able to see clearly and know why. We'll have that knowledge, and we'll understand.

Prayer

Lord, please don't let me fail the test of faith. Make me strong enough to believe you know the reason for everything that happens.

Reflection

How can I strengthen my faith today?

7

JOB'S FAITH

Job 1

Some historians believe the book of Job is very likely the oldest book of the Bible. It's the tale of a God-fearing man who suffered fearful losses—his family, his health, and his wealth. Almost everything, in fact, except his faith.

Job had a beloved family, great wealth, and a strong body to care for everything he had been given. Yet there came a time when he lost it all. All but his wife, and she doesn't exactly sound like the best of helpmeets (see Job 2:9). Or perhaps she was so devastated by the loss of her children and home that she was no longer able to function normally.

But how did Job cope? How is Job 1:22 able to record these astounding words: "In all this Job sinned not, nor charged God foolishly."

First, it appears that Job's attitude was humble before God. He fell on the ground and said, "Naked came I out of my mother's womb, and naked shall I return thither: the LORD gave, and the LORD hath taken away; blessed be the name of the LORD" (verse 21).

Even in the middle of his soul-shattering loss, Job acknowledged that what the Lord had given was also within the Lord's right to take.

Sometimes it's hard to accept that. But if I acknowledge that I belong to God and that all I am, all I have, and all those I love were given to me by him, then I know he has every right to take back what belongs to him in the first place.

Job says it this way. After his wife asked him to curse God and die, he said to her, "What? shall we receive good at the hand of God, and shall we not receive evil?" (Job 2:10).

"Shall we accept the good things God sends," Job is saying, "and not accept anything calamitous? Shall we take the blessings, but turn against him when he asks us to shoulder burdens?"

It's difficult to fathom the depths of sorrow and loss and mind-numbing grief Job experienced. It's harder still to understand how he remained strong in his faith.

Perhaps the reason is that he resolved to trust God. It was a matter of will. His own words in Job 13:15 make that clear.

The sentence rings with the depths of his faith. And we can say with Job, "Though he slay me, yet will I trust in him."

Prayer

When losses upset me, Lord, I ask to be reminded of Job. I want to say with him, "Though you slay me, yet will I trust in you."

Reflection

What loss makes me want to turn away from God?

1

JOB'S HOPE

Job 37

*I*n addition to the strong message of Job's faith that comes through in the book of Job, we learn the vital reason for Job's hope. It is found in Job 19:25-27:

> For I know that my redeemer liveth,
>   and that he shall stand at the latter day upon the earth:
>
> And though . . . worms destroy this body,
>   yet in my flesh I shall see God:
>
> Whom I shall see for myself,
>   and mine eyes shall behold, and not another.

In the midst of his intense suffering, Job knew it would pass. He knew life on earth is not all there is. He knew that his Redeemer lives and that when this was over he would stand before him and see his face. Job knew beyond all doubt that someday God would remove this suffering for all time.

Perhaps another reason Job was able to stay strong in faith, and in the hope he nurtured for a better tomorrow, was that he didn't demand to understand everything that was happening before he trusted. In fact, in the last chapter, chapter 42, he confesses his complete lack of understanding: "Then Job answered the LORD and said, 'I know that thou canst do every thing . . . therefore have I uttered that I understood not; things too wonderful for me, which I knew not'" (verses 1-3).

Life becomes easier for me also when I acknowledge that I'm not going to understand all the whys or reasons for all the losses and heartaches. It is enough to know that our Redeemer lives and that he can do anything. Even bring good out of unbelievable bad.

Sometimes the reward for trusting God and remaining strong amid relentless trials comes beyond this life. We'll understand so much better after God calls us home to him.

Sometimes God chooses to bless the faithful here and now. Job was openly rewarded before his death when God showered more abundant blessings upon his devout servant. "So the LORD blessed the latter end of Job more than his beginning" (Job 42:12).

However he chooses to do it, the Lord will always reward those who continue to faithfully hope in him.

Prayer

Lord, strengthen my faith when I remember the losses Job endured. Remind me that I can continue to trust even when I don't know all your reasons.

Reflection

How can I hold on to hope today?

2

BROKEN HEARTS, PART 1

Psalm 1; 34:18; Acts 13:22

Laverne and his brothers sometimes train horses as a sideline hobby, and they've broken some in for riding and driving.

The methods they use, although mostly similar, also vary to fit the nature of the horse. Some horses are more docile and respond favorably to all the usual training to bridles, halters, saddles, and buggy harnesses.

Others are more strong-willed. They want their own way and don't intend to change. Nor do they respond well to conventional methods of training. Then the work becomes slightly more difficult for the trainer, and a great deal more difficult for the horse.

King David of the Bible was sometimes called a man with a broken heart. But in those days, a heart that was broken had another meaning than the one that is commonly used today.

In *David: The Shepherd King*, author Phillip Keller explains that "in the Scriptures a 'broken heart' is a will that has been trained and disciplined to do God's will. The expression is used in the same sense as we speak of a horse 'being broken to the saddle' or an ox 'being broken to the plow.' . . . It means to be harnessed or yoked."[16]

King David's hardships and sorrows and regrets were used to fashion him into a "man after [God's] own heart" (Acts 13:22). His heart had been broken—which simply means it was trained and disciplined and yoked to God's will.

The horses who respond promptly and willingly to their initial training are doing a favor not only to their trainers but also to themselves. The more they struggle against the commands and the confines of saddle and harness, the more the severe the training becomes. For a horse to be of any value, it must first have its own will brought into subjection, and it must be trained to obey commands.

God wants our hearts to be broken, too, and trained and disciplined to his will. We can struggle against him if we choose, of course. But if we do, we only harm ourselves in the long run.

Prayer

If I want to be a woman after your heart, O God, I know I must first be broken to your will. Give me the grace to submit to your commands.

Reflection

How might I be broken today?

3

BROKEN HEARTS, PART 2

Luke 22:39-71

Once or twice over the years, Laverne and his brothers have encountered a horse that refused to be broken. For whatever reason, it would be a horse too strong-willed and too stubborn to respond to any of the usual or unusual methods of training, a horse determined not to submit to any authority, at any cost.

In those few cases, Laverne and his brothers had to admit defeat. A horse that can't be broken is a dangerous animal, and as such, it is almost worthless. In the end it is often resold, and frequently put down. Its own stubborn nature, its refusal to submit to any control but its own, will hasten its demise.

As people with the ability to think and reason, we can see where a horse would be much better off by submitting to its master's harness and command. But how often do we face situations where we are determined to have our own way, whatever the cost?

"There are two kinds of people," C. S. Lewis writes. "Those who say to God 'Thy will be done.' And those to whom God says, 'All right, then, have it your way.'"[17]

When I refuse to listen to God, refuse to submit to his commands, and refuse to be broken to his harness, the time will come when he will withdraw his presence from my life. In Genesis 6:3, God says, "My spirit shall not always strive with man." I understand this to mean that if I insist on my own way, God will at some point cease to try persuading me otherwise. He will let me follow the path that I, by my stubborn resistance to his authority, insist on choosing.

But I'll likely live to regret the consequences, the destination of the path, and the results of my own stiff-necked rebellion.

In verse 42 of today's Scripture reading, Jesus prayed, "Not my will, but thine, be done." The submission of Jesus to God's divine plan gave us a chance at eternal life. He yielded to God's plan. Why should we expect to do anything less?

In Hebrews 12:2, we find these words: "Jesus . . . who for the joy that was set before him endured the cross."

He knew that doing his Father's will would be far better for him than insisting on his own way.

When I stop insisting on having my own desires, and submit my stubborn will, God can at last begin to work in my life. When I yield to him and humbly say, "Thy will be done," then I am "broken" for and harnessed to God's work for God's kingdom.

And only then can I begin to discern that God's plan was far better than my own anyway.

Prayer

I know my will needs to be broken over and over, Lord. Thank you for the patience with which you work in my life.

Reflection

Where is one place I know I must still submit to God?

4

WAITING

Acts 1:1-8; 2:1-21

*M*atthan and I sat in the dentist's office, doing what those
places were designed for—waiting. Waiting until the dentist had time to see us and do an x-ray. Waiting to hear what he
would say about Matthan's repeated abscesses near a tooth with
no cavities.

Waiting is not my favorite occupation. Especially when waiting
for answers, test results, or solutions to a problem. I prefer some
activity to sitting idly by, waiting.

But frequently, God asks us to wait. Even commands us to wait.
There are times when he needs us to be still, to trust, to wait and see
what he plans to work out for us.

The disciples of Jesus might have felt the same way. Were they
impatient to begin spreading the good news of Jesus' resurrection to
the far ends of the earth? Perhaps.

In Acts 1:4, Jesus "commanded them that they should not depart
from Jerusalem, but wait for the promise of the Father."

The disciples must have felt a bit puzzled. "Lord, wilt thou at
this time restore again the kingdom to Israel?" they asked (verse 6),
no doubt wondering why they were supposed to wait when they
thought they'd be asked to go.

Jesus replied, "It is not for you to know the times or the seasons,
which the Father has put in his own power [or authority]" (verse 7).

So Jesus told them to wait. Only after they had received the
power of the Holy Spirit were they to begin their ministry in Jerusalem, Judea, Samaria, "and unto the uttermost part of the earth"
(verse 8).

We want to be up and doing, to work for God, and he asks us to wait. We pace around his waiting room, stewing, fretting, and biting nails. This time is so wasted.

Or is it? Patiently waiting for God is one way of learning to trust him. Behind the scenes, he is often working out our problems in surprising ways.

The Bible is full of promises for those who wait for God. "Blessed is he that waiteth" (Daniel 12:12). "Therefore will the LORD wait, that he may be gracious unto you" (Isaiah 30:18). "The LORD is good unto them that wait for him" (Lamentations 3:25).

Or my favorite, from Exodus 14:13-14, from Moses's words to the children of Israel as they stood upon the banks of the Red Sea while Pharaoh's army advanced behind them: "Fear ye not, stand still, and see the salvation of the LORD, which he will shew to you to day . . . the Lord shall fight for you, and ye shall hold your peace." In other words, be quiet, hold still, wait.

In essence, if God asks us to wait, he's asking us to trust that he knows best. That he knows what's going on. And that he can work it out for us, if we'll only permit him to do so.

At last the dentist showed up with the results of the x-ray. Matthan's tooth would have to be extracted. Now we wait for that appointment.

Prayer

You see my impatience, O Lord, and the way I rush into life. Show me how to slow down and learn more of you and your stillness and quiet peace.

Reflection

In what area of my life, though I would like something to happen there, is God asking me to wait?

5

THE FOLDED NAPKIN

John 20:1-18

Amazing details often emerge from the Bible when one takes the time to study the customs of those long-ago eras. Recently I came across one such custom that brought several verses in John 20 to life in a new way.

It was early on that Sunday morning after the crucifixion, and Peter and John, the disciple whom Jesus loved, were running to the sepulchre. They had been alarmed by Mary Magdalene's startling announcement: "They have taken away the LORD out of the sepulchre!" (verse 2).

Peter and John ran together to the sepulchre, but John reached it first and peered inside. Peter came too, and they stooped down, then entered the tomb. They saw the linen graveclothes lying nearby.

Verse 7 then describes "the napkin, that was about his head, not lying with the linen clothes, but wrapped together in a place by itself."

The word *wrapped* here is often translated to mean "folded." This napkin wasn't tossed aside like the graveclothes. The Bible uses a complete verse to make sure we know the napkin was neatly folded and placed aside.

Why is it so significant that the napkin was folded and laid to one side?

To understand the important meaning of the folded napkin, one must first understand the Hebrew tradition of that time. It was a custom that alluded to masters and servants, and every Jewish servant was familiar with this tradition. A servant would prepare the table with his master's food, making sure everything was perfect. Then he would wait discreetly out of sight until his master was finished eating the meal.

When the master was finished, he would use the napkin to clean his hands, face, and beard. Before he left the table, he would toss the wadded napkin upon it. Every Jewish servant knew that now he could begin clearing the table. A wadded napkin signaled "I'm done."

But if the master left the table with the napkin folded and laid beside his plate, the servant would not touch the table. In those days, a folded napkin meant "I'm coming back."

When Jesus folded the napkin and laid it aside, he was conveying a message to his followers. It said, "I'm not here now, but I *am* coming back."

Today we can read the Easter message of that resurrection chapter. And the folded napkin is our message within a message. He wants us to understand: "I am coming back."

Prayer

Amid both the mundane and the momentous of my life, Lord, I want to keep your message clearly before me. You are coming back, and I need to be ready.

Reflection

How should this message from Jesus affect my life and actions today?

6

FOR ONE SINGLE DAY

Matthew 6:25-34

Every summer in June and July, the daylilies bloom again. A single flower lasts only one day, but what grace, beauty, and color it brings to its fleeting hours! Healthy plants are usually lavish with their flowers, so the overall display lasts for weeks.

I like to take a daylily stroll each morning before beginning the day's work. I carefully break off yesterday's faded blooms and check which heavy buds are unfurling dainty petals today. Fragile and graceful and perched atop slender stems, the flowers remind me to make the most of my one God-given day. Yesterday is over; I might never see tomorrow; but I can make today beautiful.

Certainly, the daylilies waste no time with whining, complaining, or fussing. They are too busy doing what God created them to do at this season—bloom for one day.

Each year when I see the daylilies blooming with such joyous abandon, I recall the lines in Edwin Milton Royle's comical yet truthful song "Don't You Be What You Ain't," in which he points out that sunflowers don't try to be daisies, nor do melons try to be roses, so just be the best that you are.

Fortunately, my daylilies are happy to bloom exactly where I have planted them, and they do it well. For one short day, they glorify the spot I have chosen for them.

Much as I admire the daylilies, I find it very hard to live like that. Yet when Jesus said, "Take therefore no thought for the morrow" (Matthew 6:34), he wanted us to understand that he will be with us when tomorrow comes but *today* is enough for us to be concerned about today.

More often than not, I'm trying to carry tomorrow's burdens too. No, to be honest, I'm probably trying to carry the burdens of the entire week.

But Jesus said, "Sufficient unto the day is the evil [or trouble] thereof" (verse 34). He wants us to walk with him where we are, one step and then one day at a time. He asks us to bloom today in the spot where he's planted us, and not to be so concerned about where we'll bloom tomorrow—or to wonder if we'll even be blooming at all.

If and when next week or next month arrives, he will help us handle those concerns then—and not a moment sooner.

Prayer

Lord, teach me to put tomorrow in your hands, where it belongs. I can handle today, one hour at a time.

Reflection

What is one problem I can handle today?

7

A DAYLILY IN NOVEMBER

Psalm 40; Luke 23:39-43

I planted a small root of a Darla Anita daylily one year and waited with eagerness to see it bloom the next season. I like that plant partly because it shares my name and partly because the flowers are truly spectacular—a large pink-and-gold bloom with frilled edges.

However, the summer months came and went, but my special daylily had not bloomed. I was resigned to waiting another summer to see its flowers.

About October, a single flower stalk began to grow from the center of the clump. Soon buds were forming there. I would see the Darla Anita bloom after all.

But it wasn't the season for daylilies. The days were too short and chilly, the nights too long and frosty. Only one flower managed to open on the stalk. It was smaller and rather more crippled than it would have been had it bloomed at the proper time, but it was pinky gold and it was special. I took it indoors to admire for its single day.

This November daylily was extra special because I knew it had overcome some formidable obstacles to bloom in November. A daylily in June or July is lovely, but one in November is much rarer.

It reminded me of people who have also conquered formidable obstacles and begun to shine with God's love at a later day. People who have suffered cruel difficulties and insurmountable burdens yet have come to know Jesus Christ at last.

He sees every effort we make, no matter how small or feeble, and he meets us more than halfway.

The final verse of Psalm 40 says, "But I am poor and needy; yet the Lord thinketh upon me: thou art my help and my deliverer."

Even if it has taken you most of your life to come to God, he desires your heart and your worship. Just think about it: "The Lord thinketh upon you." He wants to claim you as one of his own and to usher you at last into his heaven of perfect love and peace and rest.

A November daylily is special not just because it is so rare, but also because it braved the dreary cold and bloomed anyhow.

The thief on the cross was an eleventh-hour believer, and he heard the words we all long to hear: "Today shalt thou be with me in paradise" (Luke 23:43).

It seems to me he was a November daylily too.

Prayer

O God, I want to bloom for you, wherever I am. Even amid trials, let me shine with your love.

Reflection

How could I encourage someone else today?

1

FORGIVENESS OF FLOWERS

Luke 11:1-4; Ephesians 1:7; 4:32

Along the side of one garden path, huge clumps of August Lily hostas had formed. They became more crowded every year, and more stressed. I would have to divide them or watch the centers begin to decay.

That's why I was chopping them apart with the shovel one sunny spring day. Hordes of small green points had pushed from the earth in crowded profusion, and before long a host of leaves would crush upward here. It would be better to divide the plant now and move some of it elsewhere.

With more space to grow, both the roots and the leaves would be healthier. But first came the difficult part.

Tight whorls of little leaves were chopped off above the ground as the shovel sliced through the soil. Tangled roots were yanked apart, cut off, torn away, with parts left dangling and broken. Holes exposed severed roots, and those new leaves full of potential just moments before now lay wilted. When I finished, the entire flower bed looked as if a storm had blasted through.

How forgiving flowers are, I thought as I hauled the divisions away to plant in a new place. I divide them and prune them. I chop them off and hack their roots to pieces. Yet they come back blooming, prettier than ever.

It is said that Mark Twain once wrote, "Forgiveness is the fragrance the violet sheds upon the heel that has crushed it."[18]

Not for the first time, I wished I were more like my flowers. They don't sulk, demand explanations, or complain about my terrible actions. They just settle down again, grow, and bloom.

Ephesians 4:32 sums up this attitude of forgiveness: "And be ye kind one to another, tenderhearted, forgiving one another, even as God for Christ's sake hath forgiven you."

Our sins were like the shovel, slicing us away from God. Our sins helped to nail Jesus to the cross. Yet God, for Christ's sake, has forgiven us for the terrible things we've done. Now we need to respond to God's grace by demonstrating it: turning around and forgiving anyone who hurts or harms us. There are no excuses here. No "If you feel like it, forgive." No "But if it's too hard, don't bother." No lines like "What they did was unforgivable, you're not expected to."

Just, "Forgive one another, even as God, in Christ, has forgiven you."

Even if we're torn up, bloodied, sliced to shreds. Even if our heart feels broken, exposed, and degraded.

God wants to help, if we'll let him. Maybe we can't understand why he permitted the shovel to be used when what we wanted was to continue as we were. Maybe we can't understand his reasons any better than those hosta roots could understand mine.

But he wants us to trust him. And to forgive those who wielded the shovel.

Prayer

Lord, I know you care when I am hurting because of unkind words or unpleasant actions. Help me to see what you want me to learn; help me to forgive and move on.

Reflection

What am I struggling to forgive?

2

BEARING FRUIT

Genesis 1:29; Luke 13:6-9; Colossians 1:3-6

I've been watching the apples swell on the fruit trees these last months. Once pale buds, they have grown round and smooth and red or gold. I've observed their growth as the weeks flowed on through summer. My efforts include the fertilizing, spraying, and watering. The trees' efforts produced apples.

But does it take any effort for an apple tree to grow fruit? I studied the way the small apples grow, how their stems cling fast to the branches, how the branches are firmly attached to the main trunk and the roots go deep and wide in the soil beneath.

No, I decided, an apple tree produces apples as naturally as I breathe. It doesn't take any extra effort for it to grow fruit. Because it is an apple tree, it can't help but produce those crimson or yellow globes we like to eat.

I asked myself, isn't that a picture of the kind of Christian I should be? If I am a small twig attached to the main trunk, which is God, then producing the fruit of a Christlike life should happen as certainly as season follows season.

A branch that is healthy and growing from the apple tree isn't about to grow a lot of thistles and briars. If I am serious about serving Christ as the King of my life and am attached to him by prayer, my Bible, and my church, it should be just as difficult for me to sprout thorns and prickles as it would be for an apple tree— although in my case, thorns and prickles are any works that don't bring glory to God's name.

Excerpts in today's reading in Colossians 1:4-6 read, "We heard of your faith in Christ Jesus, and of the love which ye have . . . For the hope which is laid up for you in heaven . . . and bringeth forth fruit, as it doth also in you, since the day ye heard of it, and knew the grace of God in truth."

Faith, love, and hope are mentioned here. They will bring forth fruit in us, and the growth, however small, should have begun the day we heard of God's promises and knew the grace of God and believed it all in our hearts.

It won't be in the same shape as those shiny round fruits that hang heavy on my apple trees each autumn. It will be a different kind of fruit entirely, one that forms in my heart and then reaches out to those around me in every part of my life.

And to the people around me, my fruit should be just as noticeable as that which hangs from the branches of the apple trees.

Prayer

Fill my heart with your seeds, Lord, and water them with your Word. Teach me how to bear fruit for you.

Reflection

How can I begin to grow God's fruit today?

3

PRESSING ON

Philippians 3; Hebrews 12:1

*E*very journey requires a certain amount of pressing on. No race is finished until the runners have pressed on across the finish line. And almost every day brings its own problems that demand we press on—through them or around them.

Some problems are minor. Petty, even. Those irritations and annoyances with what has been called the amazing perversity of inanimate things.

Some issues are major and involve a complete change of plans, along with a change of mind. Nothing goes as planned; we encounter not only problems but also problem people to deal with. It's very tempting to become angry and begin lashing out at others.

But that makes everything worse, not better. So we have to press on toward a better solution, a better way of handling stress.

"My brethren," says James 1:2, "count it all joy when ye fall into divers [various] temptations."

James doesn't tell us to only endure these temptations and the days when so many things go wrong that we grow upset and irritated. No, he advises us to count them as joy.

This would certainly be an enigma, except that he explains it in the very next verse: "Knowing this, that the trying of your faith worketh patience."

Evidently, James understood the importance of pressing on through the temptations that test one's faith and try one's perseverance. He knew that as we stand firmly for Christ during times of trial, our faith will be strengthened and we'll learn patience, endurance, acceptance.

In other words, as we press on through life's trials and stresses, we'll become stronger.

The apostle Paul understood the importance of pressing on, for he wrote, "I press toward the mark [goal] for the prize of the high calling of God in Christ Jesus" (Philippians 3:14).

Paul knew we would have to be tenacious day after day in order to attain our heavenly goal. He knew that pressing on in Christ would produce a strengthened faith and the self-discipline we need to successfully finish this race called life.

For only those who are persistent will reach the goal. And all those who finish the race in Christ Jesus will be the winners.

Prayer

Some days the race appears to be very difficult. Please strengthen me hourly, Lord, so that I stay focused on pressing on toward the goal.

Reflection

Where will I press on today?

4

OUR THOUGHTS

Philippians 4:4-9; 2 Corinthians 10:5

*M*atthan has never been to California, but he already knows it is a terrible place.

First, the thought of earthquakes terrifies him, and California has lots of earthquakes. Next, one of his books is about a raging fire that consumed entire neighborhoods—in California, of course. And then he found a picture of a large, poisonous lizard. "Those don't live here," Laverne assured him. "They live in dry desert areas, like parts of California."

That did it. "I'm never going to California," Matthan told me. "It has too many awful things."

A quotation from Barbara Garrison, one often seen on stickers or posters, says it well: "Fear grows out of the things we think. It lives in our minds."

Many centuries earlier, Solomon mentioned the same thing. "For as [a person] thinketh in his heart, so is he" (Proverbs 23:7).

What we feed our mind is what our mind turns around and feeds us. Thinking fearful thoughts all day long will make us fearful. Sad thoughts will make us depressed. Dwelling on everything that is wrong is enough to deject anyone.

But it also works the opposite way. Thinking of praise, gratitude, and worship or dwelling on joyous and happy thoughts will brighten one's heart and spirit. Think happy thoughts if you want to be happy.

A touch too simplistic? Yet it works. What we dwell on is what we become in our thoughts, and it spills over into words and actions.

In today's Scripture reading, Philippians 4:8 instructs us on the whereabouts of our thoughts: "Whatsoever things are true . . . honest . . . just . . . pure . . . lovely . . . of good report . . . virtue . . . praise, think on these things."

As Christians, we're commanded to "[bring] into captivity every thought to the obedience of Christ" (2 Corinthians 10:5) and to dwell on things that are pleasing to God. Obviously, when I'm focusing on things that discourage, depress, anger, or deject, I'm not focusing on the things that are positive.

If I fill my mind with bitterness or with fears, I'm just like Matthan, who has never seen the magnificent coastline of California or its mountains, forests, and parks of superlative beauty. I miss so much that is good in life if I choose instead to dwell on the terrible and the unjust.

Thoughts follow well-worn grooves in the mind, so it takes much effort and self-discipline to develop healthy thinking patterns. But no one has to do this alone: "My help cometh from the LORD" (Psalm 121:2).

God is always ready and willing to help us if we ask. Such a thought is true, just, pure, and lovely to dwell on.

Prayer

O God, help me fill my mind and heart with thoughts of you. The more I think about your love and graciousness, the less space that is left for fearful and sinful thoughts.

Reflection

What are several good things I want to dwell on today?

5

PLUGGED EARS

James 1:22; 1 Peter 3:8-12

When Alisha wants to be deliberately annoying to either of her brothers, she'll stick her fingers in her ears when they're talking to her. Not only will she plug her ears, but she will also move around and talk loudly. Anything to be sure she doesn't hear what they're saying. It's guaranteed to really irritate them.

The children of Israel, in their forty-year jaunt through the wilderness, experienced plugged ears way too often. Hearing or reading an account of their journey always amazes me. How could they be so blind, not to mention deaf and ungrateful?

But when I stop focusing on the children of Israel and turn my attention to modern-day people, myself included, I can see that we're no different. This is our jaunt through life, and quite a lot of us have our ears plugged too.

Perhaps we don't literally stick our fingers into them, but our ears are shut all too often just the same. They don't hear what God is saying to us. Or if they hear the words, the message doesn't move from the ear canal to the heart.

In the Gospels, I find that eight times Jesus instructed his followers by saying, "He that hath ears to hear, let him hear" (see Matthew 11:15; 13:9, 43; Mark 4:9, 23; 7:16; Luke 8:8; 14:35). Eight times he told us to listen to what he is saying, to hear his words, and take them into our hearts and live them.

Because hearing the words is only the beginning. "But be ye doers of the word, and not hearers only" (James 1:22). Having our ears plugged means our hearts are plugged too. If a heart is full of sin and uncleanness, that can be the reason the ears refuse to hear—or to comprehend what they are hearing.

If we continue to refuse to hear, what happens?

When Alisha plugs her ears and keeps them plugged long enough, Cody and Matthan give up and leave her alone. It's no fun talking to someone who refuses to listen.

God will eventually do the same if we turn a deaf ear to his call and his invitations and his pleadings. A day will come when his voice becomes fainter, and soon we won't hear it at all anymore, even with our ears unplugged. Then we won't be able to hear because God will have stopped calling.

But it doesn't have to be that way. We can listen to his voice and begin to respond. Each small step toward him will make the next words a little easier to hear, comprehend, and understand.

As long as we want to hear, want to know what he has to say, God will keep speaking to our heart and conscience. But he does let us decide whether to unplug our ears.

Prayer

Remind me of the ways you are speaking to me today, Lord. Help me to listen with my heart as well as my ears.

Reflection

How could I unplug my ears and really listen to God's voice today?

6

UNPLUGGING MY EARS TO HEAR GOD

Matthew 7:15-27; 1 John 2:1-17

There's an old poem my mother used to recite, "I Love You, Mother." I don't remember the exact words or the author, but I can clearly recall the message.

Each verse was about a different child in a family, and each child was saying, "I love you, Mother." But one child ran out to play, ignoring his mother's requests; another fussed and complained about her mother's decisions; a third dropped clothes and toys all over the floor.

A fourth child said, "I love you, Mother," and set about to prove it. She swept and dusted and ran errands. She willingly did whatever her mother asked.

Before skipping off to bed that night, all four children again cried, "I love you, Mother!" The poem ends with an inquiry, "How do you think Mother knew who really loved her?"

It's fairly simple, when our ears are plugged and our hearts are resistant to God's words, to be like the first three children. "I love God," we say, but ignore his clear commands. Who do we think we're fooling? Certainly not God. He's looking for far more than a bit of lip service. Jesus himself, in Matthew 7:21, said, "Not every one that saith unto me, Lord, Lord, shall enter into the kingdom of heaven; but he that doeth the will of my Father."

And 1 John 2:3 puts it this way, "We do know that we know him, if we keep his commandments."

In other words, one way to prove we love God is to keep his commandments. If we are serious about being a disciple of Jesus, it's going to take more than putting on a pious expression every Sunday and uttering some generic "God bless you" or "I love God" phrases.

Part of being a Christian is work. It takes effort. One needs self-discipline and a willingness to turn away from harmful and sinful things and habits, no matter how alluring Satan makes them appear.

I used to wonder how I could know I really loved God, but that was before I learned that love can be a verb. In fact, I believe that much of loving God comes under the category of "action verb." Remember those from English classes? Verbs do something. One doesn't sit around waiting to feel love. "For this is the love of God, that we keep his commandments" (1 John 5:3). "And this is love, that we walk after his commandments" (2 John verse 6).

If we try to keep God's commandments, the ones he left us in his precious Word, then we are loving God. It might be a struggle some days—or most days—but the harder we struggle, the greater we prove our love to be.

Each of the children in that old poem spoke the same words. Each of them wanted Mother to believe they loved her. But three of them had their ears plugged when it came to her requests. They did their own thing. Only one of those children loved their mother more than they loved themselves. It was the one who did her mother's wishes.

Prayer

Lord, to do your commands, I must open my ears and my heart and really listen to what you are saying. Help me to be willing to put your love into action.

Reflection

How can I love God today?

7

WHO ARE
THE SAINTS?

Hebrews 11:25; 2 Timothy 4:6-8

When my paternal grandfather died in the summer of 2015, he was eighty-five years old. He had built no mansions, founded no communities, led no great excursions into unknown territories. He was neither rich nor famous when he died, but he was much loved by his extended family.

He was born to a poor farmer at the beginning of the Great Depression, and he was a farmer himself until he retired. He had spent most of his life tilling the soil, earning his bread and his rest by the sweat of his brow and the toil of his hands.

He never spoke much about his faith—he just lived it. He literally chose "rather to suffer affliction with the people of God" (Hebrews 11:25) than to go against his conscience and his convictions. In a quiet way he "kept the faith" (2 Timothy 4:7), and when he died, although we missed him with death's bitter finality, we believed, as the Bible says, that there had been laid up for him that "crown of righteousness, which the Lord, the righteous judge, shall give . . . unto all them that love his appearing" (verse 8).

My grandfather was one of the people I thought about when I happened on these words: "The truly great saints are often the unknown, unrecognized, undecorated men and women whose lives reflect the love of Jesus far more than their words. These are the real saints."[19]

Sometimes the real saints say more with their lives than with their words. They aren't the ones always leading the theological

WEEK 9: HEARING GOD

arguments but are often the ones at home quietly working for peace. They are "keeping the faith" and keeping it the focal point around which their life revolves.

The real saints aren't the ones trying to convince others how right they are. Rather, the real saints are more concerned about patterning their lives after the one perfect Life, which Jesus lived. They are being his hands in a quiet way, being his feet and serving him, often in an unobtrusive way far from the spotlight of fame. The real saints are walking the faith in the simple, lowly details of everyday living rather than dreaming of some far-off day when they can do a great work for God. They know all great work is composed of many small details.

The single rebuke I remember receiving from my grandfather came when I complained that my life was not improving to any great degree. At the time, I was eighteen or nineteen, and I was wishing for more now that I was older.

He looked at me and said, "Maybe you are expecting too much."

Several decades have passed since then, but sometimes when I'm impatient with things in general, I remember his words. Maybe I am expecting too much.

If I want to live as my grandfather did, as Jesus did, I won't expect so much in the way of things. I'll be more concerned about "keeping the faith," about living as Jesus would and right where I am.

Prayer

Help me, God, to keep the faith of all your saints. Help me to live for you where I am, one step at a time.

Reflection

Who is a quiet, behind-the-scenes kind of saint I particularly admire? How can I live like that too?

1

A HEAVENLY PARENT

Isaiah 49:8-16; Matthew 5:9; Romans 8:16-18

Sue Monk Kidd writes about "the flame of joy that burns so mysteriously inside a mother's heart."[20]

Surely all mothers have felt it, that flame of joy which is the satisfaction we find in caring for our children. There's a deep contentment in feeding them, washing and clothing them, and seeing to their needs.

Of course, that's only one side of the story. The other side is the days when that flame is rudely drenched in one or more of life's floods. When the flame is put out, it can take a while to relight it.

But even when that flame of joy is feeble, even when it seems almost gone, most of us watch over our children continuously. We yearn for the best for them; we guide, train and discipline them; in addition, we care for their physical needs. Sometimes we hover and nag.

It all began the day I became a mother, that inseparable mingling of love and concern. I learned it will continue to the end of life on earth when I noticed that my eighty-plus-year-old grandmothers both still yearn over their children, my turning-sixty parents.

This is what James Dobson says: "There is *nothing* more important to most Christian parents than the salvation of their children. Every other goal and achievement in life is anemic and insignificant compared to this."[21]

That is the reason we yearn over our children, watch out for their welfare, sacrifice to nurture and support and train them. It's because we long for good things for them, the most important thing being heaven.

The way parents yearn over their children is reflected in a much vaster way in the heart of God. In Isaiah 49:15, the Lord says, "Can a woman forget her sucking child . . . ? yea, they may forget, yet will I not forget thee."

How possible is it for a mother to forget her baby? Not very likely, and yet it does happen. There are mothers who are negligent or abusive. Even those of us who aren't negligent or abusive are very human, and our children sometimes suffer from our mistakes.

But if we have become God's children, we can rest in his care. He will never forget us—our names are engraved on his hands (Isaiah 49:16). He is the ultimate parent, yearning over us, chastening us, longing to give us his best, which is heaven, if we'll only allow him to cleanse us and lead us there.

To be the children of God means yielding to his kingship and to his authority as a heavenly parent. It means surrendering our lives into his keeping, knowing that despite everything that happens here, God does want to give us his best.

And his best is better than anything we've ever been able to imagine.

Prayer

Thank you for your watchful care each night and day. Continue to guard me and keep me so that I will never wander away from you, my heavenly Father.

Reflection

How might God be yearning over me today?

2

PETER'S MISTAKES

Matthew 26:69-75

*O*f the twelve disciples, I believe I like Peter best, mostly because he's so completely human and he made so many mistakes.

He was prone to blurting out what he was thinking without considering how it would sound. That was what once earned him his sharpest rebuke from Jesus: "Get thee behind me, Satan: thou art an offence unto me" (Matthew 16:23).

Perhaps after that Peter waited awhile before he spoke again. After all, it would be a terrible thing to be speaking for Satan. For if Peter was quick to speak, he was also quick to repent. He took to heart the words of the Jesus he followed.

But the mistake for which Peter is most notorious is the moment when he stood outside the high priest's palace and insisted he didn't know Jesus. To further validate his words, he also cursed, swearing he didn't know the man now on trial for his life (and our sins).

Just a short time before, when Peter was feeling strong and confident, he had blurted out, "Lord, I am ready to go with thee, both into prison, and to death" (Luke 22:33). But when that time actually came, Peter ran. Then he denied his Savior.

Perhaps we can feel for Peter. Haven't we all, at one time or another, in one way or another, denied our Savior? Not always with words. Sometimes our actions and reactions hold no appearance of being Christlike. We can deny Christ with our words. Or with our lives.

I can look back and see too many times when I have resembled Peter. Strong one day and full of good intentions to live completely for Christ. And then failing a crucial test of Christian living before the sun set the next day.

It's good to remember that God sees our intentions and is always willing to forgive us and send us another chance if we really desire it. The message of the angel whom Mary and Mary Magdalene found at the empty tomb on resurrection morning was meant for each of us too: "Go your way, tell his disciples and Peter that he goeth before you into Galilee" (Mark 16:7).

"Tell his disciples and Peter. Make sure Peter knows." Jesus knew that the grief of Peter would be sharper and deeper than the grief of the others. He knew Peter would need an extra measure of assurance.

He also knew that Peter, despite his unruly tongue, was a disciple who would after this serve him unwaveringly.

Charles Swindoll writes: "I cannot find, either in Scripture or history, a strong-willed individual whom God used greatly until he allowed him to be hurt deeply."[22]

Sure, Peter made a lot of mistakes. When he denied Christ it seemed he was making the worst one of his life. But out of that terrible moment Peter could learn many things. And was it not perhaps the bitter memory of that denial that helped to make Peter strong enough to live for Christ every day after that? That made him such a powerful disciple? That helped him at the last, when he was also crucified, to die for the name of Jesus?

Prayer

Lord, help me to grow as Peter grew. Help me to use my stumbles and failures to make me stronger.

Reflection

How can I use a bad time to strengthen my faith?

3

PETER'S QUESTION

John 21

fter Peter had made his bitter denial, after he had wept bitter tears of repentance, he must have gotten to his feet, gathered his worn fisherman's coat around him, and gone on again.

In reading the Gospels, I find no hint that Peter used his momentary stumble as an excuse. And he could have, you know. He could have said, "All right, that's it. This whole business of being a disciple of Jesus is too hard. I give up. I'm too sinful and full of foibles."

That could have been his response. Or he could have justified his actions: "I was no worse than the others. They ran away as fast as they could, and they kept on going. If you ask me, they were denying Jesus too. So I talked out of turn again? At least I didn't do as they did and desert entirely."

Human responses, both of them. Giving up when hitting a rough spot. Justifying our sins and shortcomings.

Peter was too outspoken, perhaps, but he didn't give up. He was still there with the other disciples as they came and went during that turbulent time just after the crucifixion and resurrection. And he didn't justify his mistakes either.

John is the gospel writer who offers the most details in describing how Jesus reinstated Peter as one of his disciples. Jesus concluded his words with the instruction "Follow me."

Jesus is still calling to each of us with these words: "Follow me."

And often we still respond with Peter's question. He looked around and noticed another disciple. "Lord," said Peter, "what shall this man do?" (verse 21).

We're still like Peter. When Jesus asks us to follow him, we first look around. "Lord, what about this friend? That one? Him? Her? Do you see them? What about them?"

Jesus said to Peter, "What is that to thee? Follow thou me" (verse 22).

He's still saying that. "*You* follow me. You." Like Peter, we have to learn. We are responsible for our own soul. No one else can save our soul, and we can't save the soul of anyone else. It is Jesus Christ who saves; only as we learn to walk as he walked can we begin to reach out to others with his compassion and his love.

Peter made a lot of mistakes, but he did a lot of things right too. He spoke without thinking and he spoke too much, but he didn't give up and sink into despair. Nor did he try to justify his mistakes. He repented of them and used them to make him stronger.

Jesus would have known how it would all come out. He would have known how all Peter's words and questions could be used to mold Peter into such a faithful man of God. How even that awful moment when Peter denied knowing Jesus would be used to make him a stronger, yet humbler man—afterward.

For in Matthew 16:18, Jesus said, "Thou art Peter, and upon this rock I will build my church; and the gates of hell shall not prevail against it."

Yes, Jesus knew how Peter would be used greatly—after he had been hurt deeply.

Prayer

Lord, please use my mistakes to make me both stronger and more humble. Somehow bring good things out of bad moments.

Reflection

How has God used some of my mistakes to make me wiser and help me grow?

4

WHEN PETER WAS SLEEPING

Acts 12:1-17

After Jesus had returned to heaven, he did indeed use Peter to establish the Christian church. The first twelve chapters in Acts record the amazing growth of both the church and Peter.

There are many stories about Peter here, but my favorite is in chapter 12. It's my favorite because of a few certain words, and because of what they mean to me.

In chapter 12, Herod has imprisoned Peter for preaching about Jesus. He intends to bring Peter out to the people after Easter (verse 4).

"And when Herod would have brought him forth, the same night Peter was sleeping between two soldiers, bound with two chains: and the keepers before the door kept the prison" (verse 6).

Peter is securely locked up. There's little chance of getting out if he's chained between the soldiers, with guards before the door. Worst of all, Herod is planning to bring him out in the morning. To the people. It has an ominous sound. Does Peter have any idea what will happen then?

But he doesn't seem to be worrying. No, the text says Peter is sleeping.

There is Peter, the anxious, questioning, outspoken disciple with the foot-shaped mouth. And he's sound asleep.

To me, this seems to say he was trusting. He believed God was taking care of him and that whatever happened the next day was in the hands of his faithful heavenly Father. He's not anxious. He's not wide awake with worried eyes searching the black emptiness of a jail cell at night.

No, Peter is sleeping. I think this means he's trusting. Even in a situation from which there seems to be no escape. He's confident the God he serves is greater than the guards or Herod himself.

In a marvelous way, God has transformed a blunt and prone-to-stumble disciple into a man who's now steadier, loyal, and trusting in him. Peter has been filled with the Holy Spirit, and he doesn't deny his Savior anymore. Now he rejoices to be "counted worthy to suffer" for the name of Christ (Acts 5:40-42).

God could take Peter and use him to establish the early church not because he was perfect, but because he was willing.

God can take us too, and use us to spread his words and his message. He's not looking for perfect people; he's looking for some who are willing: willing to overcome mistakes, willing to get up when they stumble and fall, willing to speak up for Christ. And also willing to be quiet for him.

In short, willing to be hurt deeply and cleansed, and then used greatly for his kingdom.

Prayer

Please give me a heart that is willing, Lord. Willing to be used in your kingdom and for your glory.

Reflection

How could I be more willing to be used in God's work?

5

COURAGE

Joshua 1:9; Isaiah 41:10; John 3:1-21

I have read that when great storms swept across the open seas, the clipper ships of old would use the first small gust of wind to steer the ship directly into the approaching storm. Gales of such terrific force had to be met head-on to keep the ship upright.

Fear can be a great crippler, and a fearful heart will find many excuses not to take a firm stand on God's Word. It's easier to slide along with the mainstream crowd than it is to form strong convictions that are based on God's commandments.

Perhaps that is why God says, "Have I not commanded thee? Be strong and of a good courage; be not afraid, neither be thou dismayed: for the LORD thy God is with thee withersoever thou goest" (Joshua 1:9).

We're commanded to be strong and courageous. It's not a suggestion. God isn't saying, "I would advise you to be strong, and I urge you to have courage." No, he's commanding us. He says, "Don't be afraid. Wherever I lead you, I am also with you."

I greatly admire courage, though truth be told, I admire it most in other people. I'd prefer to hang back and watch what's happening before I make any move of my own.

When I was a teacher years ago, part of the package included biking four miles to the school where I taught. It was uphill about half the way, through lonely, heavily forested hills, and for most of the term I pedaled that route through the cold morning darkness.

At first, in my mind, I cranked up that hill many times at night when I should have been sleeping. Particularly if I knew I had a distasteful job ahead of me the next day. Tossing and turning and lying awake never helped much, though, and always morning came at last and I could face that hill and the hard day head-on. Reality was infinitely preferred to the futile business of trying to slink up it in my sleep at night. (I later became so used to that hill I could almost bike it in my sleep, but that's another story.)

As with the old clipper ships, when a storm is breaking, it's better to face it head-on. Tackle the unpleasantness and get it over with. Face the thing that looks like a mountain in the road ahead and climb it. Take a stand and vow to do what can be done about the hurdle in the path today.

We need the courage Nicodemus had when he came to Jesus that night to find out more about this amazing young teacher. Yes, he came in the darkness, but it took a lot of courage for him to come at all. He could have taken the easy way out and refused to listen to the inner promptings of his heart.

If a storm of great magnitude in the form of a problem is breaking over you today, don't try to slink away. It could sideswipe you and engulf you in the waves.

Meet it like the clipper ships. Head-on and with courage, because the Captain of your life has promised to be with you in the storm.

Prayer

It takes a lot of courage to live in today's world, Lord. But I know your power is not diminished, and you've promised to be with us always.

Reflection

What is one thing I'm facing where I need an extra measure of courage?

6

SMALL THINGS

Zechariah 4:10; Matthew 13:31-32; Luke 13:18-19

*M*ost of life is made up of small things. Both the mountaintop experiences and the deep valleys of despair level out to long stretches of daily living that contain neither the euphoria nor the bleakness of major highs and lows.

"For who hath despised the day of small things?" (Zechariah 4:10).

Who, indeed? Making a conscious effort to be grateful for small things opens one's eyes to the fact that they aren't small at all. They are some of God's most precious gifts.

"These are the things that made me happy today," I wrote in my journal one evening. The list looked like this:

Putting supper on the stove (after pondering Haiti's lack), and being struck with the thought that there was plenty for everyone.

Watching the fat bud stems of the amaryllis grow taller each day.

Laughing with a little boy and seeing his eyes sparkle.

An open book with a bookmark lying across its pages.

Sniffing the scent of lavender and peppermint in the lotion.

Hearing the melody of the wind chime singing through the background of my day.

Little things. But not really. All little things contribute to the tapestry of a lifetime. In the end we discover they are the big things.

Jesus compared the kingdom of heaven to a grain of mustard seed, that smallest of seeds, which grows and flourishes until at last it makes a plant that is stalwart and strongly rooted and bearing more seeds.

The kingdom of heaven begins to grow in our hearts as a small seed. If we nourish that growth, "precept upon precept; line upon line . . . here a little, and there a little" (Isaiah 28:10), God's Spirit can live in our hearts and grow into a strong and stalwart faith that no one can take from us.

Someone once wrote: "A big rushing river is but the teamwork of numberless little drops of water. A gigantic mountain is only the bulk of innumerable grains of sand and particles of dust piled up. The worthiness of the church is not expressed in terms of bricks and mortar, but in the gentle life and faithful service of its individual members."[23]

Most of the time, God isn't looking for great things from us. He wants to see whether we can remain faithful in the small things he requires of us. "He that is faithful in that which is least is faithful also in much: and he that is unjust in the least is unjust also in much" (Luke 16:10).

I've discovered that the more I'm grateful for small things, the richer and more worthwhile life becomes. Instead of despising the day of small things, we'll embrace the dailiness of life. The kingdom of heaven grows in our hearts line upon line and day upon day.

Prayer

By appreciating the little things of life, Lord, I become more aware of you. Only as I open my eyes to that which is considered small can I begin to see more.

Reflection

What are some small things I am grateful for today?

7

FAILURE AND
SUCCESS

2 Samuel 22:21-34; James 1:4-5

In some strange way, I've learned as much about being a writer from the stories that were rejected by editors as from the ones that were accepted.

And I've learned as much about being a mom from the ways I've failed and the mistakes I've made as I have from the successes.

In many ways, failure is a more eloquent teacher than success. Amos Wells would have us know: "If we have been doing our best, the failure of our work is the success of God's work in us. If we have done our full duty as prayer discloses it to us, then failure was part of our duty. God sometimes sets tasks in order that they may not be done, for the lessons of failure are far more precious than the teachings of success, and far more difficult to learn."[24]

Second Samuel 22:31 says, "As for God, his way is perfect." If we believe that God's way is perfect, we must also believe that the times we failed, despite earnest prayer and effort, also fit into his plan for our unique life.

Failure is harder to accept than success. Perhaps that's why it is able to teach so much more. From it we learn patience, humility, trust.

Nothing makes me quite so humble as acknowledging that I've failed again. Nothing teaches me patience as quickly as having to try once more. And nothing teaches me to trust God more than seeing the failure of my own goals and plans. If I'm unable to make things turn out right, it's comforting to know God has a plan and that his way is perfect.

Not only does God design our failures to bring us closer to him; in a similar fashion, he also uses the people around us to do the same. This verse by an unknown author makes it plain.

God doesn't give us the people we want—
He gives us the people we need—
To make us into the persons we were meant to be!

The reason God doesn't always give us success or surround us with people who complement us is clear in the second line—he's giving us what we *need*. In his perfect way, he knows what it will take to shape our lives and mold us into the people he wants to welcome to heaven. He's tirelessly and lovingly working to cut away our sins and the rubbish of our souls. Success won't bring us to our knees as readily as failure. Compliments won't make us turn to him as readily as criticism. Pride and arrogance disappear when we stand before him stripped of our selfish goals. Anger and grudges dissolve faster when we ask him to open our eyes to the ways we've hurt others.

There is a place for our failures in God's design for our lives.

It takes the gritty details of our lives to work like sandpaper to smooth out our rough spots. Instead of rebelling against the failures and frustrations, ask God to show you how they fit into your life.

He's got a reason for them all.

Prayer

Show me, O God, how you want me to respond to the things that go wrong in my life. When I've failed—again!—help me to get up and go on in your way.

Reflection

How do I face failure today? How do I work with a difficult person in my life?

1

SUBMISSION

Genesis 8:20-22; Exodus 29:18; Ephesians 5:1-17

As Alisha and I were baking cookies one morning, a terrible odor filled the kitchen. I rushed to investigate, certain the cookies must be burning.

The cookies were fine, but something else in the oven wasn't. I couldn't even tell what it was anymore, but whatever it had been, it gave off an awful stench as it melted into the bottom of the oven. The odor lingered a long time. We wanted to get far away from it.

For some reason, the stench brought to mind the sacrifices of the Old Testament era. In those days, when the people humbly offered their sacrifices with penitent hearts, it brought a sweet savor before God's throne. In this way he knew they were submitting to his ultimate authority in their lives.

God no longer asks me to build a fire and burn a sacrifice. Jesus was the unblemished lamb who was offered once and for all time as a sacrifice for each of us. His submission to God's plan cost his life.

We're no longer required to build fires and burn sacrifices. But our lives still bring a "sweet savor" to God. Or they stink.

Today, if we submit to God's authority, humbly and with a pure and willing heart, we're usually sacrificing some of our own desires, our selfish human natures, our anger and defensiveness. It can be even harder, mentally, to submit and relinquish those conditions of the heart than it would be to sacrifice a lamb.

The sacrifice God wants from us now is submission—submission to his authority first of all, and then to the authority he places over us. Every single person must submit to God—sometime. "For rebellion is as the sin of witchcraft" (1 Samuel 15:23).

As I understand it, witchcraft takes sin to a higher degree of seriousness because it is giving Satan the worship that belongs to God alone. And yet here God makes it plain. Rebellion is as witchcraft. Whenever I rebel against authority, I'm rebelling against God. Which is likened to practicing witchcraft.

"Submission is a challenge straight from God to you," Elizabeth George writes. "It's a measure of your spiritual maturity. . . . No one can make you submit to anyone else. You must choose to do it yourself. . . . If you aren't submitting to [authority] now, you aren't submitting to God."[25]

No matter how hard we find it to submit—to God first, then to our church, parents, husband, teachers, or the law—it must be done (except in cases of abuse or when those in authority require us to go against God's commands). The peace that follows heart-deep submission is God's way of reminding us that he has a better land waiting for those who do bow to his authority. It doesn't take much character to be proud or to oppose authority. But submission is the true test of greatness.

The sacrifices God asks us to make can bring a sweet savor before his throne if we do it willingly and with love. If he observes our submission to his authority over us, he will bless it generously.

But a wicked, rebellious, or self-serving life must stink when God observes it. And the person who refuses to submit to God's authority today will nevertheless submit before God in the next life, when it's too late to change rebellion. When it says "every knee shall bow" (Romans 14:11), that's exactly what it means. The proudest and most stubborn knee will eventually bow before God.

We can decide if we'll do it here and now while he calls us to submit. That's the sacrifice he wants, the submission he desires, the sweet-smelling aroma.

Prayer

Submission to you, God, and to others in authority is not a suggestion but a command. Show me where I need more submission in my life.

Reflection

Do I think my life smells sweet to God, or does it give off a bad odor?

2

PEACEMAKERS

Romans 12:18-21; Hebrews 12:14; James 3:18

Like most children, Matthan and his cousins Kendrick and Lavina get into a lot of disagreements. Their spats vary in seriousness, from the minor ones they resolve themselves to the more major ones that leave them in tears. Like the one that left Matthan howling through his sobs, "But, Lavina, you don't always have to have your way." Obviously, he wanted Lavina to play with him only as long as she did what he wished.

God's rules for living have been called the "if-then" commands. *If* you do this—*then* I'll do this. When Jesus says, "Blessed are the peacemakers: for they shall be called the children of God" (Matthew 5:9), he's saying, "If you are peacemakers, then you can be my children."

Most of the time we like the idea of being peacemakers. Especially if things are turning out as we want them to and people are cooperating as we'd like. Then peace isn't a problem.

One evening when Cody was seven, he and Alisha were making plans to build an elaborate pen for the puppies. A quarrel soon erupted because they disagreed about how to go about it, and at last Cody snapped, "I'm building this pen alone so I can say how it should be built. Now hurry up and help me carry these boards."

Ah, yes. As long as you cooperate with me, we'll get along fine. Being a peacemaker is not a problem. But when you start disagreeing with me, I find you're not a peacemaker after all.

It takes maturity to admit that much of the problem could be my fault. And that its solution might possibly begin with me yielding my stubbornness for the good of another.

If being a peacemaker is not optional, how can I learn to be one? How can I pursue peace? Doesn't it start with surrendering my own will and considering the plans and desires of others to be as fully important as my own? (Or even more important, for that matter.) This doesn't sound so hard, but it can be a difficult daily struggle and a lifelong task.

Phillip Keller writes in *David: The Shepherd King*, "God's people need to be reminded that disputes and quarrels that lead to evil divisions are regarded by him to be just as wicked as adultery, drunkenness, or witchcraft. . . . He has given to us his gracious Spirit of unity and harmony. Why then do so many indulge in strife and discord? There can be no blessing, no peace, no rest, no strength that way."[26]

Keller's description describes the discord of turbulent times around us today as well. But God's commands to his people haven't changed. As it says in Matthew 5, peacemakers shall be called the children of God. One way to know who is wholeheartedly following God is to look for a person who is peaceful in the chaos of a combustible situation.

Sometimes being a peacemaker means speaking up. Just as often it means being quiet. Maybe that's why we find it so hard to be peacemakers. But most conflicts would benefit from fewer words and opinions, not more. Sometimes the hardest part of being a peacemaker is holding my tongue.

The peacemakers will be called the children of God. Do I desire that enough to live peaceably with those around me?

I hope so. Because being the opposite of a peacemaker—being one who stirs up ill will and strife—means I can't be called a child of God. In the end, any amount of struggle and surrender will be worth it. For as the children of God, we'll live with him in endless peace.

Prayer

Lord, I want to live as a peacemaker during these turbulent times. Help me to know when I should speak up and when I should be quiet.

Reflection

What is one situation where I can decide to be a peacemaker today?

3

BIRTH AND GROWTH

1 Corinthians 3:1-2; 1 Peter 2:1-3; James 2:19-20

*I*t doesn't take long for a baby to be born. (At least, that is, when it's over and those grueling hours of labor are viewed from the perspective of years gone by.) But it does take quite a while to grow up.

Growing up is lengthy and time-consuming. The time from when a baby first lifts his wobbly head to the time he is finished maturing physically can take a score of years. There's so much to learn between the first tottering steps of babyhood and the fast, firm tread of young adulthood.

It also doesn't take long to be born again. To make the decision that means "Yes, I believe. Yes, I want to follow Christ. Yes, I will begin today." It takes a matter of minutes to come to that place on one's knees before God. (Or it can take years of wrestling with one's conscience before yielding. But even so, those moments of decision don't take long. I relent, I give my life and actions into God's hands, holding nothing back. I submit to his refining. The new birth has begun.)

In one sense, it takes mere moments. Yet in another, the new birth that is begun that moment usually takes quite a while to fully develop. Living as Jesus did and following in his footsteps won't be completely achieved until we stand with him in heaven. It is something we grow into gradually, one new insight at a time.

If a baby refused to take that first toddling step because there's so much yet to learn, that baby would basically be refusing to live. In the same way, if I refuse to make a beginning as a new Christian because I don't understand everything, I'm ultimately refusing life.

Only by taking a first step do we learn to walk. Only as we yield our hearts to God in faith can he reveal the next step of the journey to us. God leads step by step rather than year by year, and if we decline to take the first step, we'll never take the second one either.

Birth we didn't choose, but the new birth can be ours if we desire it. Neither parents nor pastors can give it to us, however, for each of us has to develop our own relationship with God. In the words of an old Irish proverb, "You've got to do your own growing no matter how tall your grandfather was." No one will be able to slide into heaven on the heels of godly parents or mentors. We'll have to accept the hand that Jesus offers and take those first tottering steps to him in faith before we can learn to walk beside him.

Then he will begin working in our hearts one revelation at a time, one moment of deeper understanding and then another. Little by little, year after year, he opens our eyes to all the abundance of life in his name.

There's so much to learn. And the journey will take the rest of our lives. But we have a Teacher who knows the answers, a Guide who knows the way, and a Friend who died so we could live. All he asks is that we trust him and begin.

Prayer

I never know what you'll reveal to me next, Lord, or what my next lesson in godly living will be. All I ask is that you continue to lead me as I learn.

Reflection

How can the people around me tell that I've experienced the new birth?

4

ROCKS AND CLAY
AND BRIARS

Ezekiel 11:19; 36:22-30; Psalm 40:1-3

The sloping bank on the southeast side of our house used to be a briar patch. Peter Rabbit would have been happy to call it home.

In addition to the patches of briars, weeds grew there. It was also littered with rocks that came from the hole where our basement now is. And the soil was a hard and unyielding mixture of wood, dirt, and clay that summed up a gardener's nightmare.

Rocks and clay and briars. Not much potential for a garden, but I determined to make one there anyhow.

That was more than a dozen years and scores of aching muscles ago. Today, a handful of evergreen trees are thriving along the bank. The rocks border the edge of the lawn. Masses of bulbs and hostas and ferns multiply there each season. Columbines and bleeding hearts and foxgloves reseed all over the place, and at least three different ground covers ramble sturdily toward the deeper woods.

I've pulled out the weeds and briars, left the falling autumn leaves and pine needles to mulch the areas, and replanted a few things here and there. It's not carefree, but it's fairly natural and low maintenance.

I remember the day it all began: the day I took pruning shears, a baby in the stroller, a blanket for the toddler, and went to the woods. That was the day I yanked down those first briars, which were so reluctant to leave and left bleeding scratches on my hands and arms.

There was a time my heart was full of rocks, clay, and briars of one sort or another. Then came the day I decided there was more to life than that and that if Jesus could come to earth and die for me, I could stand up and live for him.

That day I yanked the first briars from my heart. They didn't want to leave, and when their thorns raked ugly scratches across my heart, it hurt. But it was a beginning.

The rocks in my heart I removed one by one. (In fact, I'm still working at that particular chore, although they are fewer in number now.) I filled their empty spaces with fertile soil where God's good seeds had room to grow. The hard soil there began to improve. It became richer with each passing year.

Rocks, clay, and briars fill many hearts. They show up where the land is poor and barren and undernourished. But they don't have to remain. God's love, if we permit it inside, is more powerful than Satan's grip on our hearts. God's light can fill the corners and illuminate the barren places. His Word can bring fertility, growth, and fruit where once stones and thorns had persisted.

If people can create gardens out of briar patches, imagine the beauty God can create in stony hearts that were once so full of thorns.

But every garden needs a beginning. And before God can help, every heart needs that moment when it invites the Savior inside. And there's always that first briar to cut.

But the flowers are always worth some scratches. A peaceful heart that's full of love and hope at last is equally worth the pain of letting go of the harmful things.

God longs to craft a beautiful garden in your heart. But first you have to open the door and grant him entrance.

Prayer

Thank you, Lord, for the work you do in my heart. I still have a long way to go to a beautiful garden there, but together we've made a beginning.

Reflection

What is one thing I could do today to make the garden in my heart a more pleasant spot?

5

FADING FLOWERS

Psalm 33:8-9; Micah 6:8

A vaseful of lavender lilacs is drooping on the table. They have clearly seen better days and must be discarded. Their cycle from birth to bud to bloom has been completed.

It's when I go to toss those faded bouquets and catch a lingering whiff of fragrance that I remember. Fading flowers often have the sweetest fragrance of all.

Not always, but often, bouquets have a sweeter perfume at the end of their vase life than at the beginning. Spring's renewal is delightful, but the fading year offers a heady combination of colors and fragrances that even spring can't rival. Spring speaks of youth and promises and hope. But autumn symbolizes a life well lived and speaks of fruitful hours, dreams realized, goals accomplished, a learned contentment.

If flowers give their best scent just before they whither, if harvest-time brings the most colorful days of all, doesn't it naturally follow that by the last of life all those who daily walk with God will also have the kindest, most gentle personalities? That a peaceful serenity of spirit will pervade all they say and do?

I wish it would come as naturally as leaves changing colors, but instead, the older I grow, the more I learn that it takes a lot of work to attain a kind, patient, and gentle personality.

If I don't work at it now, I likely won't attain it effortlessly in a few more decades. If I let impatience, anger, discontentment, and selfishness take root in my heart, these things will certainly keep on growing until they warp me into a bitter old lady no one wants to meet or be with.

I once talked with a woman who had been a hospice nurse for many years. "People die as they've lived," she told me. "If they've been bitter and unpleasant people all their lives, they die bitter and unpleasant. But if they've been kind and unselfish and loving in life, that is how they die too."

So those sweet and patient ladies I admire, the ones who are several decades older than I am and who wear a patient and trusting expression, didn't get that way by accident. No one goes automatically from a selfish youth and a self-centered middle age to faithful, God-centered autumn years.

At last I understand that if I want a kind personality in old age, I have to begin cultivating that personality today by drawing closer to God. Jeremiah 31:3 tells how God wants to draw us to him: "The LORD hath appeared of old unto me, saying, Yea, I have loved thee with an everlasting love: therefore with lovingkindness I have drawn thee." God shows us so much love and kindness, and that is how he wants us to learn to interact with others.

As God weeds the selfishness and impatience from my heart, I can work with him to replace my sinful reactions with godly actions.

The fading flowers offer me their sweetest perfume just before they die. But that fragrance has to be within the flower all along. They couldn't proffer it at the end if it hadn't been there from the beginning.

I have to learn to choose a kind and patient personality now, one that trusts in and waits for God. If I don't, it's much more unlikely that I'll have such a personality during the autumn years of life.

Prayer

A gentle and trusting nature is learned by drawing closer to you, O God, and by struggling against my human nature. Let me show to others the same loving-kindness you have shown to me.

Reflection

How could I respond to someone more kindly today?

6

GOING OUT BLOOMING

2 Corinthians 11:20-33

*W*hen November comes, several roses are still blooming, defying the light frosts and ignoring the decreasing daylight and chilly winds. I always look at them and wonder what makes the difference between the roses that go out blooming and the ones who shrivel up and drop their leaves and petals at the first hint of cold.

I wonder the same about people. What makes one person keep on in the face of tremendous odds, conquering obstacles that would defeat a dozen others? What makes another give up at the first hint of a blustering squall and run for shelter?

The apostle Paul would certainly be one of those people who went out blooming, one who kept on despite tremendous odds. Verses 23-27 in today's Scripture reading outline some of the things Paul suffered for Christ: prison, beatings, stonings, shipwreck. Weariness, toil, sleeplessness, hunger, and cold all formed a part of his long labor. And yet he never gave up. He was still ardently serving Christ when his last days came, and he went to meet his Savior— still blooming.

When I study the roses that keep on forming buds and pushing out flowers long after others have given up because of the cold, I notice one thing they all have—a deep and thriving root system nourishing a sturdy stalk. The vast network of roots that tunnel through the soil is deep and grounded and healthy. It might be hidden, but it is still feeding those plants and making them strong enough to weather the cold temperatures.

There have been people like apostle Paul in every generation since his, people with a faith so deep that it is like burrowing roots which anchor their hearts to God. These are the sturdy people who weather storms by clinging to God rather than by withdrawing from him.

Paul's expectation might have had something to do with his ability to weather storms. He expected to suffer for Christ, so it was no surprise to him when it occurred. He was not demanding an easy life or heaven on earth. He knew being a Christian in his time meant being required to suffer for it.

Am I a soft Christian today, expecting God to solve my problems and give me an easy way to heaven? If I am, my roots don't go very deep. No wonder I give up at the first hint of frost.

Or am I like the roses that wedge their roots deep into the soil and stand up sturdily—blooming till the end? Am I expecting to suffer for the name of Christ if I must, rather than giving up when the difficulties arise or searching for an easier side road to glory?

Jesus suffered greatly to pave the route to heaven for me. Why can I not suffer for him? And not only suffer, but also blossom for him as long as I can—and then go to meet him, still blooming.

Prayer

I long to stand strong and bloom for you, Lord. But I can only do that if my roots go deep into the soil of faith and trust.

Reflection

How can I grow deeper into God's Word today?

7

REST

Leviticus 25:1-5; Matthew 11:28-30; Hebrews 4:1-11

*W*hen I found myself standing in the middle of the living room wondering why I was there and what I was looking for, I suddenly understood my mom so much better.

As a girl, I didn't know how it was possible to forget what you were seeking before you got to the next room. When it happened to Mom sometimes, I'd think, "She must be aging remarkably fast." I couldn't believe it might happen to me someday.

I didn't realize it at the time, but the years of our youth inhabit a very small length of time. Every additional year of life adds more responsibilities, bills, names, acquaintances, work, repairs, things needing your attention. There's so much more to do, so much more to remember, and so many more people making demands on your time. Life can become a whirl lived in a whirlwind of haste. No wonder a middle-aged brain blows a fuse occasionally and forgets what it was supposed to remember.

God knew we needed rest. A night's sleep to recharge our batteries between the days. A day of rest and worship to begin each week. In the Old Testament, even every seventh year was set aside to be a year of rest for the land (see Leviticus 25). It seems to me that God never intended us to charge at life as if we had to get it before it gets us. He planned for us to have decent intervals of rest and rejuvenation.

"Come unto me," Jesus invites, "and I will give you rest. Take my yoke upon you, and learn of me; . . . and ye shall find rest unto your souls" (Matthew 11:28-29). Here Jesus twice promises rest if we'll only come to him, give him our sins and burdens, and learn to abide in him. He wants us to slow down, to make room for him, and to understand that a life lived too fast loses much of its peace.

An anonymous writer penned these words: "Returning to solitude, that meadowland for hearts, allows fruit to be borne, for fields left fallow to rest, yield richest harvest."

That was why God created a day of rest, a year of Sabbath, and night for repose. If we don't take time for rest and refreshment, if we burn out completely, the harvest will suffer. We won't just stand in the middle of the room wondering what we're doing there; we'll neglect to care for our souls and the souls of our children.

In a world full of increasing chaos and turmoil, the balance of rest can be hard to find. Some seasons of life are incredibly wearying, and rest seems illusory. Mind and bodies are stretched thin, the responsibilities of family, mortgage, and business as well as home and church and school are a daily juggling act. Then the promise in Hebrews becomes especially beloved: "There remaineth therefore a rest to the people of God" (4:9).

Hebrews 4 is a challenge to enter into God's rest, and it sums up what should be the reason for all our work: "Let us labour therefore to enter into that rest" (verse 11).

If rest seems fleeting and illusory here, and our brains are stressed out by trying to keep up with the demands placed upon them, that verse puts everything back into its proper perspective.

Our most important job is work that takes us closer to heaven, God's peaceful, stress-free home. He has created eternal rest for all his people.

Prayer

Heavenly Father, thank you for the rest you've promised. When life feels out of control today, remind me that some things can wait but that spending time with you and caring for my family can't.

Reflection

How can I decide what's most important for me to do today?

1

TAILS IN THE TOILET

Exodus 20:1-17;
Matthew 5:27-28; 18:34-35; 1 John 3:15

Autumn arrives, and with it come creatures moving indoors. Their numbers are legion, and they like to claim our home as theirs.

Some of their proliferation must be due to our mountain home. When you live deep in the woods, it is to be expected that the wildlife will be more abundant than the people. And that they have fewer inhibitions about inviting themselves indoors.

Spiders hog the corners, crickets love the basement, and roaches ride along in on the firewood. Bugs and beetles and flies like to hibernate in the trim around the windows and doors. Spraying only accomplishes so much. It's a frustrating battle as I struggle to get rid of them all.

One fall day I was cleaning the bathroom. I scrubbed the toilet and flushed it, and a long, wet, skinny gray tail slithered down into the bowl with the water. It was not my best moment.

After Laverne took care of the mouse that had found refuge in the toilet, I went on cleaning. It's a task that is never really complete, for there are always more bugs and ants (and mice) somewhere in the forest who are searching for lodging.

The worms and beetles sneaking inside remind me of all the sins and impurities that want to come creeping into my heart. It's a greatly frustrating battle as I struggle to get rid of them all.

I've read that most sins can be classified as sins of the flesh or as sins of the spirit. Most of God's Ten Commandments teach against the sins of the flesh: idolatry, stealing, murder, immorality, lying. God wants his people to live lives that are upright before him.

For those of us who've grown up in a sheltered and secure environment rooted in home and church, and who've had godly parents to go before us and shield us and give us biblical training, those sins of the flesh don't pose as much of a problem. Early discipline helps a lot.

But before there's any chance to feel smug, we come to the sins of the spirit. These are just as apt to test the strength and scruples of a Christian. Jesus spoke against the sins of the spirit in no uncertain terms when he warned that hating others is murder in our hearts, that adultery in the heart is adultery just the same, that harboring unforgivingness, bitterness, and grudges are all sinful, and likewise all pride and arrogance.

Sins of the spirit are heart conditions. Jesus condemned those along with the sins of the flesh. If I despise another soul who is created in God's image, I'm guilty of murder. If I'm full of pride, I'm elevating myself above others and above God. If I won't forgive another person, God won't forgive me either.

The Pharisees condemned the sins of the flesh, but their hearts were proud and equally full of sin. For although sins of the spirit can be hidden, they will keep us out of heaven just as certainly as sins of the flesh.

Sins creep into my heart in much the same way bugs creep into my house. It's to be expected as long as we live in a fallen world. I can see I'll be in a battle against both as long as I live, and I have to loathe the presence of sin as much as I loathe seeing a tail in the toilet.

Prayer

Lord, I know you despise the sins that sneak into my heart as much as I despise the bugs and mice that sneak into my house. Please help me to despise the sins as much as you do.

Reflection

What sins of the spirit are sneaking into my heart today? How can I get rid of them?

2

TREASURES

Proverbs 24:1-4; 1 Timothy 6:6-10, 17-19

A story in *God's Little Devotional Book* tells of a farmer who had lived on the same farm all his life. It was a good farm, but as the years passed, he became dissatisfied. Every season he discovered more things he disliked about his farm, and at last he called a real estate agent and asked to have his farm placed on the market. When it was sold he would move on to find something better.

The real estate agent arrived and walked across the farm, preparing a description of it. Before he printed the advertisement, he called the farmer and read the ad aloud. The list of advantages was long: fertile fields that produced abundant crops, healthy cattle, barns in good repair, wide meadows, good water supply, and a two-story house. This, he said, was how he would advertise the farm, and since it was prime land, it should sell fast.

"Wait!" cried the farmer before the agent hung up. "I've changed my mind. I don't want to sell. I've been looking for a farm like that for a long time."

Wealthy business magnate John D. Rockefeller was once asked, "How much does it take to satisfy a man?" His reply? "A little more than he has."

Harboring a critical and discontented attitude is a sure way of forgetting our blessings. It is only as we practice gratitude that our eyes are opened to all we really have.

Proverbs 15:6 reminds me, "In the house of the righteous is much treasure." Here, in our homes, is the real treasure God has given: love, harmony, and joy; the children who are a "heritage of the LORD" (Psalm 127:3), and a haven from life's storms. Instead of becoming critical and disillusioned about the things that are wrong, I have a choice. I can work to improve them while being grateful for what is right.

"You create the atmosphere of the home with your attitude," author Elizabeth Elliot once said.[27] Kashena Violet adds in a poem, "Your perspective is a lot of your attitude / and your attitude will control your thoughts / and your thoughts will control you."[28]

What we see depends a great deal on what we're looking for. Sometimes we're a lot like the farmer who decided to sell his farm because he saw only the negatives. The positive things were there too, but he couldn't see them as long as he focused only on what was wrong.

The atmosphere in our home reflects our attitude just as surely. The whole family often absorbs the attitude of the mother, which places a lot of responsibility squarely on her shoulders. Do we see our family as our treasure? They'll pick up that attitude. Or do we view them as a burden, a stumbling block in the way of our selfish desires? They'll absorb that too and react accordingly.

In the end, we usually find what we're looking for, and life gives us back what we put into it. In the words of nineteenth-century poet Hester Cholmondeley, "Still as of old / men by themselves are priced— / For thirty pieces Judas sold / Himself, not Christ."[29]

When you become dissatisfied and critical, when you go to sell the farm, be careful. You might be selling yourself instead.

Prayer

Teach me to look at life with eyes wide open, O God, and to value the treasures of home and family and church. For a critical and discontented spirit doesn't come from you, nor does it glorify you.

Reflection

How can I cultivate a grateful attitude for what is right in my life?

3

THE PATH OF PAIN

Isaiah 48:10; Zechariah 13:9; Malachi 3:1-5

Years ago, pastor George Matheson wrote,

My God, I have never thanked Thee for my thorns. I have
thanked Thee a thousand times for my roses, but not once for
my thorns. I have been looking forward to a world where I shall
get compensation for my cross: but I have never thought of my
cross as itself a present glory. Teach me the glory of my cross:
teach me the value of my thorn. Shew me that I have climbed
to Thee by the path of pain. Shew me that my tears have made
a rainbow.[30]

Pain has a way of reducing life to its core and showing us who we
are and what's really important. It can lead us to God if we permit
it to.

I read about Dr. Lambie, a medical missionary to Africa, who
learned from the natives how to ford the many swift and dangerous
streams in that often bridgeless land.

The danger in wading the streams came from the threat of being
swept off one's feet and carried into deeper waters and drowned
or killed upon the rocks. The Africans showed Dr. Lambie how to
select a stone, the heavier the better, and heft it on his shoulder. As
he crossed the stream, the stone served as ballast by keeping his feet
planted firmly on the riverbed.

This rock Dr. Lambie likened to the burdens we carry through the
dangerous stream of life. They keep us firmly anchored to God while
temptations swirl around us.

The pain and hardships can draw us closer to God. They are
similar to the refining process that gold has to go through in the fire.

Struggles give us a chance to grow, a chance to rid our souls of the impurities that would separate us from God, and a chance to develop our faith.

God wants to draw us closer to him and to soften our proud hearts, and frequently the furnace of affliction teaches us more than the calm, sunny days. "Behold, I have refined thee, but not with silver; I have chosen thee in the furnace of affliction" (Isaiah 48:10).

The path of pain can lead us up the mountain, can bring us closer to God. But the path of pain can also drag us down into anger and bitterness. If that is how we react to burdens and struggles, we'll eventually be pulled down into depression, desperation, deep emptiness.

Then each person must decide whether to stay in the valley, wallowing in mud, or to climb, slipping and stumbling perhaps, but still pressing upward. Poet Daniel Crawford gives us a reminder: "There is no high hill but beside some deep valley. / There is no birth without a pang."[31]

We'd all prefer the airy heights of the mountain to the dark sorrow of a deep valley. But we seldom leap to a mountaintop in a single bound. To get out of the valley, we have to begin climbing— one faltering step at a time. We have to keep on going even if we slip backward every few steps. No one can be refined without pain. Little good can be born in our souls without first experiencing the sharp birth pangs.

Just as burdens can be the rocks that keep us anchored firmly to faith in God, the pathway of pain can be used to make us more like him. Poet Helen Steiner Rice put those thoughts into words: "No one knows God or sees Him as plain / As those who have met Him on the pathway of pain."[32]

Prayer

Dear heavenly Father, I want to use my pain as a path that leads me closer to you. Show me how to use the valleys as a starting place.

Reflection

What is a valley in my life today? How can I begin climbing out?

4

COUNTERFEITS

Matthew 4:1-11; 2 Timothy 2:14-19

As the perennials grow and spread, I'm often left with huge clumps to divide. Friends have learned to stay away in spring if they don't want me trying to give them plants. If anyone so much as shows her face, I'll probably try to find a way to foist some green and growing thing upon her.

One year early in my garden venture, I found several small rosebushes volunteering for duty in my flower beds. Despite their contrariness, I love roses, and I hadn't known they would reseed. So these miniature bushes were welcomed. I admired their distinctive rose leaves and wondered what color they would bloom.

"Here's a little rosebush," I told a friend one day as we, armed with shovel and pots, walked along paths and searched for plants for her flower beds. "I don't know what color it will be, but you may have it, if you like."

Certainly she liked. We dug it out and she hauled it home. Later that year I achieved enough horticultural knowledge to realize two things. One: roses don't reseed. Two: those rosebush look-alikes had a striking resemblance to an ugly, prickly, and hated multiflora rose-bush that was growing to mammoth proportions in another corner of our property.

I have since, I think, lived down the humiliating memory of the day I dug out that counterfeit rose for my friend. I assume she has also forgiven me for so misleading her.

But it reminded me how often Satan counterfeits God's love and divine plan and promises people many things if only they'll serve him as the prince of their world. His imitations are passed off as genuine, but Satan comes with the intent to deceive, and by the time we realize that his glittering promises conceal many death snares, we've already fallen for his lies.

Studying the Scriptures and keeping our hearts in line with God's words, as well as heeding the still, small whisper of our conscience, makes us less susceptible to Satan's counterfeits. We learn that the roses he would like us to believe are genuine will quickly flourish into ugliness that invades our hearts and grows by evil leaps and bounds.

If Satan can't foist his lies upon us, he has another method of luring us away from God. In C. S. Lewis's words, "If you examined a hundred people who had lost their faith in Christianity, I wonder how many of them would turn out to have been reasoned out of it by honest argument? Do not most people simply drift away?"[33]

The seeds of Satan's imitations begin as the tiniest of suggestions, a sibilant whisper today and again tomorrow tempting you with something he assures you doesn't matter. But the more aware we become of his counterfeits, the easier they are to spot.

Don't become discouraged when you discover Satan has deceived you. Just turn around and rush back to God as fast as you can. He knows those who are his, and he rescues all those who call on his name. He delivers us out of countless temptations.

"Nevertheless the foundation of God standeth sure, having this seal, The Lord knoweth them that are his. And, let every one that nameth the name of Christ depart from iniquity" (2 Timothy 2:19).

Satan's cheap imitations soon tarnish and sicken. But God's genuine love promises to eventually bloom into a fragrant and beautiful rose.

Prayer

Show me where I might still be believing some of Satan's lies, O Lord. Show me where his deceptions might be making inroads in my heart.

Reflection

Am I listening to any of Satan's counterfeit promises? How can I tell?

5

MASTER AND KING

Matthew 7:21-27; 16:24-28; 1 Peter 5:6

esus Christ came to be our Savior. But he cannot be our Savior
unless we put him on the throne as the Master of our life.
Through the spiritual valleys of life, when problems would
willingly capsize our faith, it's comforting to remember that Jesus
is a Savior who has promised his disciples a home in a land that
is problem free. We love to focus on being an adopted child of the
King who will reign forever. "Jesus, [who] delivered us from the
wrath to come," says 1 Thessalonians 1:10. We gladly claim him for
our Savior.

But sometimes we forget the other side of the coin, the second
blade of the scissors.

"Jesus Christ is not only Savior," writes Oswald Chambers in *He
Shall Glorify Me*. "He is King, and He has the right to exact anything and everything from us at His own discretion. We talk about
the joys and comforts of salvation; Jesus Christ talks about taking
up the cross and following Him. . . . Jesus Christ is Savior, and He
saves us into his own absolute and holy lordship."[34]

When we accept Jesus Christ as our Savior and expect him to
save us "from the wrath to come," it's wise to also realize that this
means making him the Master of our entire life, not only the convenient bits and pieces we'd like to turn over to him.

Just as the two blades of a pruning shears can't be separated and
still function as a shears, so we can't separate the Savior of Christ
from the Master of Christ. If we try to accept him as our Savior
without acknowledging him as our Master, we're like those whom

Jesus mentioned in Matthew 7:21: "Not every one that saith unto me, Lord, Lord, shall enter into the kingdom of heaven."

It's possible to hear God's Word, to believe that Jesus is the Savior, and still not humbly submit to his authority as Master.

Verse 21 concludes with Jesus adding, "But he that doeth the will of my Father which is in heaven [shall enter heaven]." That is the difference.

If Jesus is our Master, we expect to do his will. Someone once noted, "Many people want to serve God, but only in an advisory capacity." Unfortunately, those are the ones who want a Savior to take them to heaven but not a Master to serve while here on earth.

Sometimes when I'm trying to work out a problem and I'm praying about it, I realize it sounds as if I'm trying to advise God. Then I have to remember a question I read one day. It's good to periodically ask it of myself. "Do I serve God, or do I expect him to serve me?"

There's a difference. And he is my Savior only as I submit to him as my Master.

Prayer

I want to take up my cross and follow you, Lord, and I long to submit completely to your kingship and to your authority in my life. As my Savior, you have a perfect right to ask anything of me.

Reflection

Is Jesus the Master and King of my life, as well as my Savior? How can I tell?

6

WINDING LANE

1 John 5:4-5; Revelation 21:23-27

ur winding country lane, tucked away in the hills of southern Ohio, seems to have escaped the touch of time. It could just as easily be wandering through the forest of a century ago.

This lane is nearly a mile long. It splits from a gravel road and begins its rambling journey to our home through level stretches of fields and pastures.

Then the scattered trees thicken, and soon it ventures into the woods, dipping into little hollows, climbing the small hillocks, curving along the side of the mountain. Sometimes you arrive at a bend in the lane and can't see what's ahead because the trees grow thickly there, and sometimes you can look down the mountainside and see trees growing in the valley.

If you're not sure of your destination, you might begin to fear you're lost in the boondocks. If you don't believe someone really lives back here, you might turn around and go back the other way. There are some places where the lane seems to be wandering aimlessly to nowhere.

Life reminds me a lot of our lane. The beginning is fairly level and doesn't require much effort. But like our lane, life becomes more complicated and requires more effort the further you go. Life is full of ups and downs too, valleys where we sink and hills where we climb. There are rocks to stumble over, and sometimes a poisonous copperhead brings us up short.

Then there are the bend-in-the-road places where only the next few steps are clear, and maybe not even those. It's only as we struggle past that fearsome bend that we can see what's on the other side.

And sometimes the next part is even rockier and the hill even steeper than we'd anticipated.

But the lane is only the journey. It leads to our home, and when we arrive we forget the twists, the bends, the hills, the valleys, the rocks and stumbles. The windows are full of light, the kitchen is full of food. Everything we love is here, and the lane is forgotten.

Life is like that too. It's only our journey to that heavenly home God has promised his sons and daughters. Yes, it can be a difficult trail. Sorrow and trials and loss are a sure part of it, and it's certain we'll all come to places where we can't see what's ahead, places where we want to give up and turn back, and places where rocks and snakes cause alarm and dread.

But when we arrive home at last, the journey will be forgotten. God's light and love will fill our hearts as well as our heavenly home. The trail will not have been too long or too difficult. Because we will be home. And nothing else will matter.

Prayer

Heavenly Father, when the lane of life seems especially hard, remind me that it's only the journey. The destination will be worth every twist and turn.

Reflection

Am I at a level spot in my life's journey now, or am I on a hill?

7

A SERVANT'S HEART

John 13:1-16

*E*arly each spring, melting snow and frequent downpours muddy the long lane that winds through the woods to our home. By late summer, dust billows up from the wheels of vehicles; puffs in tiny clouds follow our feet. Pavement sounds pretty good at those times.

The roads in Galilee where Jesus and his disciples walked from town to town were surely no better. One can easily imagine that they too were thick layers of dirt. And the shoes in those days were often a single piece of leather fastened to feet by narrow strips wound around ankles and toes. If Jesus and those with him were wading through mud or dust all day, their feet would have been particularly grungy by nightfall.

And then one evening Jesus shocked his little band of tired disciples when he fastened a towel around his waist, filled a basin with water, and began to wash their filthy feet.

I've read that in those days not even a Hebrew slave could be ordered to wash someone's feet. It was a dirty job, and one that no one would be expected to perform for another person.

It's easy, then, to understand why Peter refused. "Thou shalt never wash my feet" (John 13:8). Peter the outspoken was likely speaking for all the appalled disciples. They didn't want Jesus to so demean himself. It was not appropriate that the One who was the Teacher and Master should wash his disciples' feet.

But Jesus came to serve. He had a pure servant's heart that was humble and so full of love for those around him that he would wash their filthy, calloused feet and dry them with a towel. And then he would walk to Golgotha and die for them.

"A new commandment I give unto you," Jesus told them that evening when their feet were dry and clean. "That ye love one another; as I have loved you. . . . By this shall all men know that ye are my disciples" (verses 34-35).

Here *love* is used again as a verb, and not as some warm feeling. It is a love that will forget self and reach out to help someone else. Love will sacrifice for the needy, care for the unlovable, clean up the dirty. It will stoop to do the lowliest jobs in the most humble of settings. It will wash the feet of those around it. In many and various ways.

The way we love and serve those around us is a clear picture of how well we love and serve Jesus. "As ye have done it unto one of the least of these . . . ye have done it unto me" (Matthew 25:40).

Prayer

Show me how I could serve you better, Lord. Show me where I should stoop to wash another's feet.

Reflection

How can I have a servant's heart today?

1

SUCH AS WE JUDGE

Matthew 7:1-5; Romans 2:1-12

Could you turn the pages?" Matthan asked me as we sat on the recliner looking at his book. "I want to use my hands to hold my ears shut."

I stopped chewing my apple. "Do you want me to sit somewhere else?"

"No, no." He stuffed his fingers in his ears. "You page." He wanted to continue reading the story with me beside him, as long as he didn't hear me crunching my apple.

Matthan is unfashionably blunt. "I don't like to sit beside you," he once told his little cousin at Grandma's table. "Your nose is too messy."

Matthan isn't only blunt; he's just like the rest of us. He sees others' faults clearly and his own through a glass darkly. His nose is often messy too, and he chews loudly.

Jesus told us that we'll surely be judged with the same judgment we use on others (Matthew 7:2), and yet we go right on judging. Sins look so much more serious when someone else is committing them, but when I'm the guilty one, I can find all manner of lame excuses to justify my actions. And that looks far more serious to God than it looked to me when Matthan was concerned about Wesley's messy nose and didn't realize his own was running.

Someone once noted that the sins and shortcomings and faults we find most glaring and offensive in others, the ones we consider hardest to forgive, are the ones we have a problem with in ourselves. How thoroughly we dislike being reminded about our sins. How defensive we become when someone points out where we need to do better. And yet how much we see where those around us need improvement!

The book of Romans has been called the apostle Paul's greatest work, and here in chapter 2, he minces no words. If we judge others and yet do likewise, we are really condemning ourselves. God alone has the right to judge.

"But we are sure that the judgment of God is according to truth" (Romans 2:2). God knows the truth about everyone's struggles toward righteousness, and he will judge accordingly. "Shall not the Judge of all the earth do right?" (Genesis 18:25).

We're here not to judge one another but to help one another. Our job is to follow Jesus, to show his love to others in the way we love, help, and react to them. We can point out that it takes repentance, sorrow for sins committed, a new life that's born in Christ, and one that has forsaken sin. But judgment of the rebellious and disobedient isn't in our hands. God makes that clear in Hebrews 10:30-31: "'Vengeance belongeth unto me, I will recompense,'" saith the Lord. And again, 'The Lord shall judge his people.' It is a fearful thing to fall into the hands of the living God."

So judgment is not in our hands. And if it's in our hearts, we'd better tackle that sin too.

Author Lisa Harper writes, "Christians have to recognize that Christ alone has the perfect combination of righteousness and compassion to stand in judgment of the human heart. The only One worthy of condemning us chose instead to pardon us."[35]

God could condemn us all. He has the perfect right. But he would far rather pardon our sins, if only we are willing to kneel before him and ask for that pardon.

And if we are his and are cleansed in Jesus' blood, even God won't judge us.

Prayer

I need your pardon so often, God. When I see how far short I fall from being who I should be, I lose all desire to judge those around me.

Reflection

How could I be more loving and less judgmental today?

2

CHILDREN AND GOD'S CHILDREN

Isaiah 11:6; Matthew 18:1-6; Mark 10:13-16

Five children are running through the house yelling to each other. They bang through the doors and leave them open, inviting flies inside. Their noise makes it hard to think, much less write, and I tell them to go outside. "Ride your bikes or play on the trampoline," I say.

Silence descends, an empty one. Just me shuffling around in a silent house, listening to a fly buzz against the ceiling.

In the stillness, I recall an oft-quoted line from President Theodore Roosevelt: "No other success in life—not being President, or being wealthy, or going to college, or writing a book, or anything else—comes up to the success of the man or woman who can feel that they have done their duty and that their children and grandchildren rise up and call them blessed."[36]

Build a house and you'll eventually leave it behind. Castles crumble and mansions burn. Use your life to establish businesses or accumulate vast wealth or achieve fame—and in several decades it will likely all vanish from the face of the earth.

Invest your time in the life of a child, and the results have the potential for eternal rewards. "Empires fall, mansions crumble, cattle die, and machinery rusts away. But a child lives on and on in the lives of descendants and in the lives of those he influences, all the way into eternity."[37]

Jesus loved children when he walked on earth, and he gladly welcomed them into his presence. He still loves all the children all over the world. He longs to bring each one into his Father's heavenly kingdom.

But we grow up, we lose a child's trusting heart, we become skeptical and cold and proud and bitter. We build walls around our souls or become rigid or unrepentant or self-righteous. So much of what Jesus loves in a child's innocent heart is gone.

Yet it doesn't have to be so. We can consciously choose to become a child of God, a trusting, humble child who depends on the heavenly Father. In fact, we really have no choice if we want to live for God. For Jesus said, "Except ye be converted, and become as little children, ye shall not enter into the kingdom of heaven" (Matthew 18:3).

The children question my decisions occasionally and quarrel with one another and their playmates. They need chastening and lessons in honesty and unselfishness and love. In our relationship I see a parallel that often reminds me of my relationship with God. He has to keep guiding me, teaching me, and chastening me, and sometimes it takes a long time for me to learn a single lesson. Just as I love my children and want the best for them, God loves each of his children. He wants what's best for every single one of us too.

But that best is seldom achieved without some pain and learning and struggle. And then the difference between children and adults becomes more apparent.

Children normally submit to the loving authority of their parents. And each person who belongs to God will submit to him and his Word. The one who doesn't belong to him will refuse.

Prayer

You are a heavenly Father watching over your children, just as I watch over mine. Guide me and keep me from wandering into places where I don't want to go.

Reflection

How can I prove that I am one of God's children?

3

WHERE SAFETY IS

John 10:22-30; 1 Peter 5:8

Thick, thorn-flecked canes of a climbing Peace rose grow over the wooden frame of the garden swing. The new leaves are large and green, and buds are forming on all sides. And behind the thorny canes, near the center of the lattice, a chipping sparrow has built a nest.

There's safety for her five tiny fledglings in that nest. Safety in the secure circle this mother bird has woven for a shelter and a home.

As long as the baby sparrows remain in the haven behind the long rose canes, they will be safe. But as soon as they begin to venture away from that ring, they will be in danger.

Cats prowl the paths and hawks fly overhead. Sometimes a snake slithers along beneath the crowded plants. Things that would like to dine on baby birds come and go.

God has a safe place for you and me too. As long as we remain in the center of his will, he can protect us.

But sometimes, headstrong and disobedient, we'd rather have our own way. Perhaps we can't see anything to fear; perhaps seeking God's will doesn't seem as important as the things we desire.

But as soon as we leave the safety of God's will for us, danger increases "because your adversary the devil, as a roaring lion, walketh about, seeking whom he may devour" (1 Peter 5:8). God's protection is very necessary because he sees so much further and knows so much more than we do.

If God is guiding us and we are walking within the circumference of his will for our lives, then his authority protects us. The devil's power is limited when God's hand is resting upon us.

Just as the little sparrows' safety is in their sheltered nest, Jesus assures us our safety is in God's hand. "My Father . . . is greater than all; and no man is able to pluck [my sheep] out of my Father's hand" (John 10:29). We're safe there, and what's more, no one will ever be able to snatch us away from that safety.

I repeat, no one can snatch us out of God's hand. But one person can make us decide to willingly leave that safety—oneself. By deliberately ignoring his warnings, by willfully choosing disobedience, we at length wander away from that protection. We become like sheep without a shepherd, easy prey for hungry wolves and coyotes. And the devil knows exactly when that happens. He's prowling about, seeking to deceive anyone who has turned away from God's hand.

But if God is at the center of our life and we are at the center of his will, we can rest securely in his shelter. During the sunshine and the storms, he will be with us and will keep us in the canopy of his hand.

Prayer

Lord, when I see the mother bird caring for her babies, I think: that's how you want to care for me. Please prevent me from walking away from you.

Reflection

Am I resting in God's will for my life today?

4

HARVEST

Genesis 8:22; Revelation 14:14-19

Harvest comes with every year. Long ears of corn thicken on the browning stalks, heavy blackberry clusters drag the canes downward, grapes begin purpling on the vine, pumpkins swell orange, apples dangle from the branches. It's time to bring in what was planted, cared for, fertilized.

"Could we pick strawberries on other plants too?" Matthan asked me one day when we were looking for ripe berries.

"No, they only grow on strawberry plants," I replied. "If we want strawberries we have to grow that kind of plant."

Harvest follows the natural course God set in motion when he created the world. You can plant thistles and pray for watermelons if you like. God could make a thistle plant grow watermelons, of course, but he probably won't. If you plant thistles, you will very likely harvest thistles too.

The natural world is still rolling along in its orderly pattern, with fruit yielding fruit, vegetables yielding vegetables, and weeds yielding weeds. If you want a certain harvest, you're going to have to plant a certain seed.

To some extent, the spiritual world follows the same sowing and harvesting pattern. We can't control our circumstances, but we can shape our attitude. And our attitude is what does much of our spiritual sowing.

For instance, if I sow a lot of anger and bitterness in my spiritual life, I probably shouldn't expect to harvest a crop of gratitude and joy. It's only when I consciously decide to cultivate a thankful and pleasant attitude that I can expect to harvest such a crop.

If I sow arrogance and cruelty, I shouldn't expect to harvest kindness. And if I indulge in sin and all kinds of sinful practices, I can in no way expect to gather in a harvest that includes a close relationship with God, pleasure in his company, or the comfort of his love, guidance, and care.

Johann Wolfgang von Goethe, a German poet born in the mid-1700s, wrote a poem called "As a Man Soweth."

> We must not hope to be mowers
> And to gather the ripe gold ears,
> Unless we have first been sowers,
> And watered the furrows with tears.
> It is not just as we take it,
> This mystical world of ours,
> Life's field will yield as we make it,
> A harvest of thorns or of flowers.[38]

But one thing about life, which is God's field, is that it's never too late to begin planting good seeds. If we're alive and desire it, we can begin a new crop that's sown in love, peace, and forgiveness.

God is the Master Gardener of the human heart, and it's never too late for him to work a miracle there.

Prayer

God, you are the Master Gardener of my heart. I need your help to plant the kind of seeds that will yield a heavenly harvest.

Reflection

What am I planting in my heart today? What am I harvesting?

5

THE STORY OF
TWO APPLE TREES

Proverbs 24:10; John 15:18-25

I planted two dwarf apple trees, a red and yellow delicious, one on each end of the flower beds near the front door. They grew splendidly the first year, and each one filled its space as a sturdy little tree with branches that grew strong and healthy and rustled with deep-green apple leaves.

The second summer was a summer of storms. After some especially forceful winds and downpours, the golden delicious lay on the ground by morning. It had snapped off at the base near the graft.

I dragged the little tree away from the spot where it had been planted and wondered what made the difference between the two trees. What enabled one to bend while the other broke? Why could one sway before the turbulence of the wind, bend before it, and yet rise again, while the other gave in and broke off?

Why do the winds of adversity that howl through every life cause one person to break before the gale while another rises above it? How can I learn to bend with the storms until they pass instead of breaking in the gales of discouragement that would bid me turn aside from what I believe?

Possibly there are many answers. The one that helps me most is to lower my expectations. Instead of thinking I have a right to an easy life, I remember that two thousand years ago, Jesus told his disciples, "In the world ye shall have tribulation: but be of good cheer; I have overcome the world" (John 16:33). And two millennia have not changed that.

Life is full of various tribulations. No surprise there. Yet many of us persist in thinking we're supposed to coast into heaven on a smooth and easy road.

There are many places to coast to, but heaven isn't one of them. Yes, Jesus' blood gives you and me the chance to go there, but now that his part of the deal is done, we still must fulfill our part. Tribulations come to test us, try us, strengthen and refine and purify us. One writer explains it this way: "Trials and hard places are needed to press us forward, even as the furnace fires in the hold of that mighty ship give force that moves the piston, drives the engine, and propels that great vessel across the sea in the face of the winds and waves."[39]

Adversity certainly tests the Christian's faith. But prosperity is an even greater test. When everything is going well, we somehow lose that dependency on God. Thomas Carlyle said, "Adversity is hard sometimes on a man, but for one man who can stand prosperity, there are a hundred that will stand adversity."[40]

Prosperity is a deadly foe because it lulls us to drowsiness in its luxurious lap. It closes our eyes to our need for God while it dulls our senses. But adversity brings us face-to-face with our own frailty. It makes us realize that if we don't have God, we're lost. No matter how much we shrink from adversity, we need it to make us strong and to help us prove our faithfulness.

As the apple trees demonstrated, there are two ways to face storms. We can give up and break. Or we can cling to Jesus and ride out the storm, bending before him in faith and trusting prayer.

No matter what comes, we have the privilege of saying with Job, "Till I die I will not remove mine integrity from me. My righteousness I hold fast, and will not let it go: my heart shall not reproach me so long as I live" (Job 27:5-6).

Prayer

There is much adversity in every life, heavenly Father. Please show me how to use it to grow stronger and more loyal to you.

Reflection

How am I facing today's storm: by bending or by breaking?

6

PRUNING BACK
THE FOREST

Psalm 18:36; Proverbs 4:12; 1 Peter 2:21-22

*W*e built our home into a mountainside covered with trees, brush, and green briars. Basically, we chopped out an area of wilderness and placed a bit of civilization within it. Briars crowded as close as we permitted them.

Born into me, for some reason, was an urge to plant, weed, garden, and dig in the soil. I set about making a garden in this wilderness, which was the place I had come to call home. It was at once wearily demanding and highly elating.

The gardens I was making were rewarding as they grew, but for every inch of ground I took from the forest and mountain around me, several more inches were revealed. Bit by bit I pruned back the forest, but always there would be more to do. Unless I plan to landscape entire mountainsides—which I don't—I will never be finished.

I encountered a similar situation in my spiritual life. My heart was full of the thickets and briars at one time; when I began pruning in there, so much more was revealed that needed to be pruned. For every sinful thought and habit I yanked out, God showed me another that needed some attention when it was exposed to his Word and will.

Sometimes we're tempted to look at the Bible and say, "There's so much in here I don't understand. Why even try?"

The truth is, I'll never understand everything. But I do understand enough to begin, which is admitting that I'm a sinner who needs

Jesus' blood and God's grace or I'm lost for eternity. Then I begin studying the Bible. And as I go, the way will be opened, step by step.

God could open our eyes all at once to everything he wants us to learn. But it usually happens step by step and inch by inch as we read and study and discover new ways of applying his Word to our life. Most often, we prune back the tangle of sin and wrong reactions and attitudes and thoughts one small bit and one small victory at a time.

We must take that first step that's clear to us before God will show us what's next. In the same way that life is lived hour by hour and day by day rather than all at once, so our spiritual life needs to follow a step-by-step pattern. The second step won't be revealed until we take the first.

It has taken me years to prune back the forest around our house to the point where I have it now. And if I were to relax for even one season, briars would come creeping back and small trees would take root and begin to grow where they shouldn't. It takes much surveillance.

My heart is the same way. If I relax my vigil, selfishness creeps back in—plus greed, pride, anger, and so much else that is wrong.

Pruning back the forest doesn't happen in a day. Neither will I learn everything I need to know about living a Christ-filled life all at once.

But step by step and inch by inch. It's amazing what one can do just a little bit at a time.

Prayer

Show me what I should work at in my heart today, Lord. Show me what I should prune out next.

Reflection

What is one small step toward a better relationship with God that I could take today?

7

LIFE'S CROSSROADS

Isaiah 40:18-25; Hebrews 13:7-17

*O*ur property terminates at the edge of a mountain. It really
seems to be the end of civilization. But if you wade through the
underbrush and angle down off the mountain, you come to a road
and buildings in a surprisingly short time.

What marks the end of our property is the start of someone else's
land. What we see as the conclusion, someone else sees as the beginning. The difference is simply in how we view it.

Sometimes we encounter days that seem like endings: God has
placed a period where we'd like a comma to be. But just as often,
what we view as the end is really a beginning after all.

It's like a large pink ball my children once played with. Greenish-
gold lines circled it, wrapping all the way around, and there was
really no way to tell where a line began or ended. There was only
perspective. The part we looked at could seem to be the end of that
particular line. Or the beginning.

God has no beginning or ending, for he has always been and
always will be. "It is he that sitteth upon the circle of the earth" (Isaiah 40:22). He can see both the dawn and the sunset of our lives.

But since we can't, we frequently come to places that look like the
end. The end of hopes, goals, and fondly cherished dreams. We lose
loved ones, homes, jobs, possessions. Life screeches to a halt and
revolves around loss. This is the end, we decide.

But then life tilts to a new start, in the same way a ball rolls, and
the circle shifts. We wade through the underbrush of grief that clogs
our personal mountain and find another road and buildings, a different set of goals and dreams. Closer to us than we would have believed.

If we walk with God on this road called life, the bends won't seem quite as alarming because we can trust that he knows what's on the other side. The places that appear to be dead ends don't have to seem so bleak because he already knows what the new beginning will be.

If we're trusting God instead of our own resources, we can say with certainty, "Jesus Christ the same yesterday, and to day, and for ever" (Hebrews 13:8), and we can know he is beside us, unchanging.

It takes faith to see an end as a new beginning instead. But nothing is too hard for God, and he sees the entire circle that's our life. He has designed the bends too. He knows which new beginnings will cause us to walk toward him and heaven's dawn.

Prayer

Lord, it's comforting to believe that you are watching over the endings and the beginnings of my life. May each new start find me closer to you.

Reflection

Am I at an ending or beginning in my life today?

FAQS ABOUT OLD ORDER MENNONITES

The Author Answers

1. ARE YOU AMISH?
Because of our plain dress, horses, and buggies, most people assume we are Amish. But there are also many Old Order Mennonite communities throughout the United States and Canada. Customs vary from one group to another. Old Order Mennonites drive horses and buggies, and also dress and live according to the guidelines of their communities.

2. WHAT IS THE DIFFERENCE BETWEEN AMISH AND OLD ORDER MENNONITES?
In the way we interpret the Bible, not so much. We both believe the Bible is the inspired Word of God, that all people are guilty before God and need to repent of and forsake sin and obey God's Word. As far as I'm aware, all groups agree that baptism should happen upon one's confession of faith, and that nonconformity to the world and nonresistance are important, to name a few distinctives we have in common.

In the way we live and dress, the differences are a great deal more varied. The simplest way I've found to explain to someone how to tell the difference is that most Amish men have a beard while most Mennonite men are clean-shaven, but that depends on the community. Among women, the fabric of Amish ladies' dresses is one solid color while many Mennonite ladies wear dresses made of patterned fabric.

3. WHAT DOES THAT WHITE CAP ON YOUR HEAD MEAN?

It is a prayer covering. We believe 1 Corinthians 11:3-16 explains that women should wear a covering while praying, and since we are told to "Pray without ceasing" (1 Thessalonians 5:17), we wear one all the time, except when we sleep at night; then we wear a small kerchief.

4. DO ANY MENNONITES OR AMISH BELIEVE PLAIN CLOTHES WILL TAKE THEM TO HEAVEN?

No. Jesus' blood, his forgiveness, and his love is what will open the door to heaven for all his people. All the plain churches I know of teach the new birth; faith in Jesus Christ as the Son of God; love for God and fellow humans; and obedience to God's commandments as the way to heaven.

Some books I've read do portray the plain people as believing their conservative way of living is how they will enter heaven. I have never met any Amish or Mennonite person who actually believed that. As far as I know, our conservative dress code is for modesty, nonconformity, to show our church affiliation, and to dress in a way which "becometh [people] professing godliness" (1 Timothy 2:10).

5. ISN'T IT HARD TO LIVE AS YOU DO?

Hard is relative, and I don't consider my way of life difficult. If I ever find a certain point difficult, it usually stems from my own attitude and not my way of life at all. There's joy in submitting to God's plan for my life! I can honestly say I have never seen anything in modern society for which I would willingly trade what I have. My life revolves around faith in God and love for him, my church, and my family. None of us are perfect; we need God's forgiveness as much as anyone else. But there's a strong center to my life as part of a Christian community, and I would have it no other way.

NOTES

1. Source unknown.
2. Charles Wagner, *The Simple* Life, trans. Mary Louise Hendee (New York: McClure, Philips, 1904), 55.
3. C. S. Lewis, *The Problem of Pain* (New York: HarperCollins, 2015), 91.
4. James Dobson, *When God Doesn't Makes Sense* (Carol Stream, IL: Tyndale House, 1993), 83.
5. Ibid.
6. Phillip Keller, *David: The Shepherd King* (Waco, TX: Word Books, 1986).
7. Oswald Chambers, *Shade of His Hand* in *The Complete Works of Oswald Chambers* (Grand Rapids, MI: Discovery House, 2000), 1223.
8. Thomas Carlyle, "Lecture V: The Hero as Man of Letters: Johnson, Rousseau, Burns," in *On Heroes, Hero-Worship, and the Heroic in History: Six Lectures* (London: James Fraser, 1841), 285.
9. Paraphrased from Elizabeth George, *Loving God with All Your Mind* (Eugene, OR: Harvest House, 1994), 200.
10. Ibid.
11. Darlene Marie Wilkinson, *The Prayer of Jabez for Women* (Colorado Springs, CO: Multnomah, 2002), 39.
12. Barbara Holland, preface to *Endangered Pleasures* (Boston: Little, Brown, 1995), xii.
13. Oswald Chambers, *The Moral Foundations of Life* in *The Complete Works of Oswald Chambers*, 732.
14. Oswald Chambers, *Our Brilliant Heritage* in *The Complete Works of Oswald Chambers*, 955.
15. Dobson, *When God Doesn't Make Sense*, 17.
16. Keller, *David: The Shepherd King*, 183.
17. C. S. Lewis, *A Year with C. S. Lewis: Daily Reading from His Classic Works* (Harper San Francisco, 2003), 374.

18. Although this line is frequently attributed to Mark Twain, evidence suggests that the original author may well be unknown.

19. Larry R. Valorozo, title unknown, *Adventist World*, April 26, 2016, 45.

20. Sue Monk Kidd, "I Don't Want to Be a Mother Today!" (n.p., n.d.).

21. Dobson, *When God Doesn't Make Sense*, 199.

22. Charles Swindoll, *Come before Winter and Share My Hope* (Grand Rapids, MI: Zondervan, 1985), 154.

23. Source unknown.

24. Amos Wells, *Little Sermons for One* (Boston: United Society of Christian Endeavors, 1898), 36.

25. Elizabeth George, *A Young Woman after God's Own Heart* (Eugene, OR: Harvest House, 2003), 97.

26. Keller, *David: The Shepherd King*, 164.

27. Quoted in Elizabeth George, *A Woman after God's Own Heart* (Eugene, OR: Harvest House, 2006), 143.

28. Kashena Violet, "Most Times I Forget," *Beginnings* 16 (publication of adult student writing of the Ohio Writers' Conference, n.d.), 80.

29. Hester H. Cholmondeley, "Betrayal," in *Baker's Pocket Treasury of Religious Verse*, comp. Donald T. Kauffman (Grand Rapids, MI: Baker Books, 1980), 136.

30. Quoted in Swindoll, *Come before Winter*, 489–91.

31. Daniel Crawford, *Not Lawful to Utter: And Other Bible Readings* (New York: Hodder and Stoughton, 1914), 110.

32. Helen Steiner Rice, "The Way to God," in *A Collection of Faith, Hope and Love* (Uhrichsville, OH: Barbour, 2012).

33. C. S. Lewis, *Mere Christianity* (New York: Touchstone, 1996), 125.

34. Oswald Chambers, *He Shall Glorify Me* in *The Complete Works of Oswald Chambers*, 516.

35. Lisa Harper, *Stumbling into Grace* (Nashville: Thomas Nelson, 2011), 133.

36. Theodore Roosevelt, *The Foes of Our Own Household* (New York: George H. Doran, 1917), 256.

37. Source unknown.

38. Johann Wolfgang von Goethe, "As a Man Soweth" no. 318 in *742 Heartwarming Poems*, comp. and ed. John Rice (Murfreesboro, TN: Sword of the Lord, 1964).

39. A. B. Simpson quoted in L. B. Cowman, *Streams in the Desert* (Grand Rapids, MI: Zondervan, 1997), 199.

40. Thomas Carlyle, "Lecture V: The Hero as Man of Letters," in *On Heroes, Hero-Worship, and the Heroic in History*, 314.

ABOUT THE AUTHOR

*D*arla Weaver is an Old Order Mennonite mother of three children; she writes regularly for *Family Life, Ladies' Journal, Young Companion,* and other periodicals directed primarily to Amish and Old Order groups. She is also the author of *Many Lighted Windows* and *Until the Day Breaks.* Darla and her family live in southeastern Ohio, where Darla especially enjoys gardening, the inspiration for many of her devotionals.